The Life and Words of
JOHN F. KENNEDY

By James Playsted Wood

and

The Editors of COUNTRY BEAUTIFUL Magazine

Published by Country Beautiful Foundation, Inc., Elm Grove, Wisconsin
Distributed by Doubleday & Company, Inc., Garden City, New York

COUNTRY BEAUTIFUL

CONTENTS

The Life and Words of JOHN F. KENNEDY

Cover illustration by Olindo Giacomini

DEDICATION

To the young people of America. May they examine the life and sacrifice of President Kennedy and follow the example of his devotion to his family, his country and the cause of peace. This book is also dedicated to Jacqueline Kennedy and her children. May they continue to be our guide and joy.

The Editors of COUNTRY BEAUTIFUL Magazine

The President "is a vital force in maintaining the independence of his country," Mr. Kennedy said. He is pictured with Lyndon B. Johnson who succeeded him as President of the United States.

JOHN F. KENNEDY: In Memoriam

John Fitzgerald Kennedy's contribution to his country will unfold, as President Lincoln's did, with the passing of time. Every young American felt the spirit of his life and the tragedy of his death.

As President he had but three short years in office, but in that time he presented to the world a picture of America as a youthful, outward looking nation ready to help men everywhere solve their problems and preserve the peace.

He had a special meaning to American youth. He proved that the younger generation has a special contribution to make to the nation, and it was his hope that our young people would develop their talents to the fullest.

John F. Kennedy is gone, but his radiant example should inspire each of us to achieve and accomplish great things.

LYNDON B. JOHNSON
THE WHITE HOUSE
August 1964

INTRODUCTION

JOHN F. KENNEDY'S CHALLENGE TO THE YOUTH OF AMERICA

The youngest man ever to be elected President, John Fitzgerald Kennedy, had a special feeling for young people. He invariably saved his most challenging statements for student audiences, for he believed that peace and brotherhood and progress were possible only if the young people of the world faced the future with hope and enthusiasm.

His appeal to young men and women grew out of his approach to life. For him each day was a new adventure. During his three years as President perhaps the most durable gift he gave to the American people was the idealism and excitement he brought to public life.

Nothing was closer to President Kennedy's heart than the idea that every child should have a full opportunity to develop his talents without being held back by prejudice or poverty. He wanted the youth of this country to have the best schooling possible—and he was equally concerned that they learn to love and to conserve the American land itself.

Some of our Presidents have had unusual interest in nature and the out-of-doors. Perhaps our most enthusiastic outdoorsman-President was Theodore Roosevelt: His adventures included cowpunching in the North Dakota Badlands country, the famous cavalry charge up San Juan Hill during the Spanish American War, the exploration of the upper Amazon River and a big game safari to East Africa. During his seven years in the White House Theodore Roosevelt created many new national parks, stopped the destruction of forests and fought to save the buffalo and wildlife.

Another President who took a deep interest in conservation was Franklin D. Roosevelt. Although polio paralysis kept him from being a rugged outdoorsman, he always had a special feel for the land. As a private citizen he planted over 50,000 trees on his Hudson River estate, and as President he launched bold new programs to harness our rivers, to replant our forests and to halt the waste of soil erosion.

John Fitzgerald Kennedy also had a special love for the out-of-doors. As a youngster at the summer home of his family on the Atlantic Coast, he formed strong ties to the sea and the seashore. The skills he developed as a swimmer and sailor probably saved his life when his patrol boat was sunk in the far Pacific during World War II.

President Kennedy wanted every boy and girl in America to have a chance to enjoy the out-of-doors. He feared that our conservation failures were

The President and Mrs. Kennedy loved children. He once called the talent of youth
"a resource which must not be wasted."

everywhere reducing opportunities to appreciate natural beauty and to have rugged contact with rivers and woods, with wildlife and wilderness.

As United States Senator he worked hard to save the great outer beach of Cape Cod as a National Seashore for all Americans. As President he favored action on a broad front to save enough outdoors for the citizens of tomorrow.

John Fitzgerald Kennedy's work was cut short by a tragedy, but the goals he set are still before us. This book is a message to you from President Kennedy, for his words challenge all of us to get in the fight to keep our country beautiful, and to give each American a full opportunity to excel and to achieve.

STEWART L. UDALL
WASHINGTON, D.C.
July 1964

JOHN FITZGERALD KENNEDY
President of the United States of America
January 20, 1961—November 22, 1963

HERITAGE

OF A

PRESIDENT

America's Presidents have come from widely differing backgrounds. George Washington was born to estates in colonial Virginia. Abraham Lincoln was born in a log cabin in the backwoods of Kentucky. Thomas Jefferson was a Virginia gentleman. Andrew Jackson was a product of the rude South Carolina frontier.

John Fitzgerald Kennedy, son of a multimillionaire father, was born to great wealth and secure social position. His first American forebears had been Irish immigrants who fled the potato famine of 1847 to settle in Boston, but behind him were two generations of affluence and political success in city and commonwealth office.

One grandfather, Patrick J. Kennedy (1863–1929), was an East Boston saloonkeeper who served five terms in the Massachusetts House of Representatives, then was elected to the Massachusetts Senate. He became in turn Boston's Fire Commissioner, Street Commissioner and Election Commissioner. A quiet man, Patrick J. Kennedy, who eventually owned three saloons, a wholesale liquor business, a coal company and a share of the Columbia Trust Company, controlled the vote in East Boston.

John Kennedy's other grandfather, his mother's father, John Fitzgerald (1863–1950), attended the famed Boston Latin School which Benjamin Franklin, Ralph Waldo Emerson and his brothers, Henry Adams and many other eminent New Englanders had attended. After his graduation he became a clerk in the Boston Custom House, where Nathaniel Hawthorne had once worked.

As talkative as Patrick J. Kennedy was quiet, John Fitzgerald flung himself into Boston politics, becoming Democratic ward leader in a part of the North End of Boston, councilman, alderman, state legislator and, in 1910, mayor of Boston. "Honey Fitz," "The Little General," "The Little Napoleon," was a 5-foot 2-inch bundle of blarney, energy and song.

John F. Kennedy had those qualities which he believed necessary for a good President—"moral courage, a sense of the future, a sense of the past, a physical vitality, intellectual vitality, intellectual curiosity and purpose."

*President Kennedy's
grandfather Patrick J. Kennedy,
politician and businessman.*

*John F. Kennedy was born on May 29,
1917, in this three-story frame house on
Beals Street in Brookline, Massachusetts.*

He would give a political speech to any group in any place at any time. He would sing "Sweet Adeline" with gusto and gestures to audiences in Boston or in South America, as he did when President Franklin D. Roosevelt sent him there on a goodwill tour.

Joseph Patrick Kennedy, son of Patrick J., was ambitious and determined from boyhood. At 9 years of age he was selling candy and fruit on chartered steamboats that left Boston harbor packed with men, women and children on riotous political excursions. At 15 he organized a neighborhood baseball team, named it "The Assumptions" after the parish church, hired a ball park and sold 3,000 tickets at 25 cents each to what he advertised as a championship game.

When, like Honey Fitz, he entered Boston Latin, Joseph P. Kennedy had little time for studies. He was manager of the football team. Twice he was elected captain of the baseball team. He was cadet colonel of the school's regiment. He won the Boston high school batting championship. The trophy for this had been donated by Boston's mayor, Honey Fitz, and young Kennedy was already courting his daughter Rose, then a student in Dorchester High School.

From Boston Latin, Joseph P. Kennedy entered Harvard in 1908. Again his grades were low, but again Joseph Kennedy became a big man on campus. He made two college clubs and joined a fraternity. He became captain of the Harvard baseball team. Popular and an athlete, big Joe Kennedy was still fiercely ambitious. He liked to win. He scorned losers, and he did not intend to be one at Harvard or later.

During college vacations he and a classmate ran sightseeing buses to nearby Lexington and Concord, where the first battles of the Revolutionary War had been fought. They took in almost $5,000, a huge sum of money then. Joseph Kennedy wanted more. As soon as he graduated, he got into banking as a state bank examiner at $125 a month. He stayed two years in the job. In 1914 the Columbia Trust Company was in financial trouble. He borrowed $45,000 to buy stock in it and at the age of 25 became one of the youngest bank presidents in the country.

That same year Joseph P. Kennedy and Rose Fitzgerald married, uniting the two most powerful families in Boston politics. It is indicative of the standing of the two families in the Irish Catholic community in Boston that Rose and Joe were married by William Cardinal O'Connell in his private chapel. The wedding was a splendid affair. The couple honeymooned at the exclusive and expensive Greenbrier in White Sulphur Springs, West Virginia, then returned to a home which Joseph Kennedy purchased on Beals Street in the Boston suburb of Brookline.

During World War I, Joseph P. Kennedy resigned his bank presidency to become assistant manager of a plant of the Bethlehem Steel Company. He went on from this to head a Boston investment banking house, to buy partial control of a chain of motion picture theaters in

Joseph and Rose Kennedy posed for a family portrait in 1934 with eight of their nine children. Pictured are (front, l. to r.) Patricia, Mrs. Kennedy, Edward, Mr. Kennedy, Kathleen, Eunice, Rosemary, (rear, l. to r.) John, Jean and Robert. Joe Jr. was not present.

. . . I grew up in a very strict house, and one where there . . . were no free riders, and everyone was expected to . . . give their best to what they did. . . . There is no sense in trying to do anything unless you give it your maximum effort. You may not succeed, but at least the effort and dedication and interest should be there.

Television-Radio Program, "Presidential Countdown:
'Mr. Kennedy: A Profile,' " (CBS), Sept. 19, 1960

About 50 years ago, an Irishman from New Ross traveled down to Washington with his family and, in order to tell his neighbors how well he was doing, he had his picture taken in front of the White House and said, "This is our summer home. Come and see us." Well, it is our home also in the winter, and I hope you will come and see us.

New Ross, Ireland, June 27, 1963

New England, to become a Wall Street financier whose dealings in stocks piled millions on millions of dollars for him. He dealt in big city commercial real estate and made more millions. Just before prohibition was repealed he obtained import licenses for Scotch whiskies and made still more millions in this venture.

During World War I, Joseph P. Kennedy had met Franklin D. Roosevelt, then a vigorous young Assistant Secretary of the Navy. Kennedy became a strong supporter of President Roosevelt and his New Deal in the 1930s and was rewarded with high offices and responsibilities during the long Roosevelt Administration. In the fall of 1937 he was appointed to the highest diplomatic post the President had to offer. He was made United States Ambassador to Great Britain.

Joseph P. and Rose Fitzgerald Kennedy had nine children. The first was Joseph P. Kennedy Jr., born in 1915. The second was John Fitzgerald Kennedy, born May 29, 1917. The others were Rosemary, Kathleen, Eunice, Patricia, Jean, Robert and Edward.

JOHN FITZGERALD FRANCIS KENNEDY

The first school John Kennedy attended was a private day school, the Dexter School, a few blocks from his home in Brookline. He never went to a public school.

Jack lived in the shadow of his brother Joe Jr. Joe was two years older. He was larger, stronger, better looking and the boss. He announced that he was boss, and he maintained his position with his tongue and with his fists. As the Kennedy family grew, Joe promoted himself to a sternly enforced leadership of his brothers and sisters, provoking both the admiration and exasperation of his younger, often sickly and more bookish brother Jack.

The family had a big, white summer home at Hyannis Port, some 75 miles southeast of Boston, on the outer or ocean shore of Cape Cod, and a palatial winter home in fashionable Palm Beach in Florida. Wherever they were, Jack Kennedy wanted to be everything that Joe was. He wanted to run and fight and swim and sail, to play baseball and football, as well as Joe did. If Jack was never able to outclass Joe in anything but swimming, it was not for lack of trying, and when they were small boys the fights between them were frequent and furious.

Their father encouraged competition among all his children. Unceasingly ambitious, ruthlessly competitive, intent always on financial and social gain, Joseph P. Kennedy wanted his sons and daughters to be as vigorous and as purposeful as he. With the others, Jack Kennedy was expected to put forth every effort in every game. The Kennedys played for keeps. Losers got nothing, not even sympathy. To do less than one's best was a disgrace.

Jack Kennedy, though small and frail, was an eager member of the Dexter football team.

Joe Jr. (right), who was killed during World War II, was Jack Kennedy's boyhood ideal.

Their mother, gentle and extremely religious, saw to the spiritual upbringing of her large family. Her life centered in her Church, and she strove to make all of her sons and daughters as devout as she.

Their grandfather Honey Fitz delighted in all the children but especially in the two older grandsons. He played with them, made political speeches for them, sang "Sweet Adeline" for them, took them to Boston Red Sox baseball games. He was always running for some office. He was campaigning unsuccessfully for governor of Massachusetts in 1922 when Jack was 5 years old. He took the small boy with him as he campaigned, displaying him happily to his henchmen and political cronies on the streets of Boston's wards.

The Kennedy children grew up with sports and games, with religion, with politics all intermixed. Both parents encouraged lively dinner table discussions and arguments about current affairs. Jack Kennedy was aware of the national and international news as well as of the waters of Nantucket Sound, the crack of bat against ball, the jar of a football thrust into his chest seconds before onrushing Joe crashed him to the ground and he leaped up again.

To be nearer his Wall Street center of operations, and to have his family grow up in a more liberal and democratic atmosphere than as Irishmen and Catholics they could know in conservative and puritanical upper-class Boston, Joseph P. Kennedy moved to New York. He rented a private railroad car to transport all of them from Brookline to their new home in Riverdale, just north of New York City.

Jack Kennedy attended fourth, fifth and sixth grades in the Riverdale Country Day School and continued there after the family moved into an 11-bedroom red brick mansion on Pondfield Road in Bronxville, a wealthy Westchester County suburb. Nurses and servants looked after home and children. There were wide lawns with big trees. The lawns were ideal for touch football, but the trees were a hazard in the games they played with all their might. Jack often emerged scratched and bruised from the fight.

He was a Boy Scout now, concerned with woodcraft, camping and hiking, as well as games and sports. He went on overnight hikes, one of them as far away as West Point on the Hudson River. This new

---

. . . Those societies that have produced great creative and political achievements have almost always given a high place to the physical vigor of the individual citizen. For it is only upon a foundation of individual hardiness and vitality that we can build an "exercise of vital powers along the lines of excellence."

"Physical Fitness: A Report of Progress" an
article in Look Magazine, Aug. 13, 1963

A firm believer in education, Mr. Kennedy also stressed physical fitness, for he said young people "must have an opportunity for physical development as well as for intellectual growth."

17

status brought him problems as well as pleasure. Knapsacks, blankets, a canteen and a poncho cost money. The tenderfoot was forced to ask his father for a 30-cent increase in his weekly allowance of 40 cents.

When he was 13, Jack Kennedy left home for the first time. He was sent to Canterbury School, a Catholic school run by laymen, in New Milford, Connecticut. It was sports, not studies, that attracted the new boy. Joe was a natural athlete. Jack was not, but he was eager and a fighter. Practice bored him but, with his long and hard experience among his brother and sisters behind him, he was tigerish in a game. Football at Canterbury was fine with Jack Kennedy. Latin and French were not. He was a little homesick too.

The two things he seems to have wanted most at this time were to equal his brother Joe's feats as an athlete and to eat all the chocolate cream pie he could get. Once at Hyannis Port, tempted beyond discretion, he ate his own piece, then snatched up Joe's, crammed it whole into his mouth and fled. Joe raced out of the house after him threatening everything from a black eye to a broken head. The whole family chased after him to save the criminal from the pursuer's wrath. Jack was about to dive off a stone sea wall into dark and dangerously swirling waters when Joe, convulsed by the sight of his younger brother's terrified face smeared with whipped cream, laughed and relented.

Jack's marks at Canterbury were poor. Though his spelling was bad and his paragraphing clumsy, he did fairly well in English. In the spring term Jack was stricken with appendicitis. An immediate operation was performed, and he spent the long summer recovering at Hyannis Port.

Everything always seemed better at Hyannis Port. Swimming, sailing, softball on the lawn, racing the sandpipers along the beach, even sitting on the curbstone in Hyannis eating an ice cream cone while he waited for the family car to pick him up after a shopping spree with his brothers and sisters, was happiness. He could wear the oldest shorts, shirts and sweaters he could find with no one to object. He could spend all day in the salt water or just fooling around with the family's boats. Friday nights there were always 25 or 30 boys and girls—neighbors and friends—in to see the latest movies in the family projection room in the basement of the Kennedy house. Well and happy again, he wished the summer would never end.

Sailing is the sport at which Jack Kennedy excelled. When he was at Harvard, he and another student won the intercollegiate yachting championship over nine other colleges, and as a young Senator, he often sailed with Mrs. Kennedy off the coast of Massachusetts.

JACK (KEN) KENNEDY, CHOATE '35;
PRINCETON EX- '39; HARVARD '40

In the fall, Jack Kennedy entered The Choate School, a distinguished preparatory school with a typical New England elm-shaded hillside campus, in Wallingford, Connecticut. Joe—big, poised and a brilliant student—was already a popular football, baseball and hockey star. Immediately, Jack, who had to make up for his older brother's natural skills by sheer determination and will to win, went out for football.

He was too light and too frail for the school squad so he had to content himself with playing hard on his class team. He became a Choate cheerleader. He won a pie-eating contest. He became a leader in after-lights-out bull sessions, for he loved to argue and, once he was convinced that he was right, he would never change his mind. Though in those days it was sometimes mistaken for stubbornness, Jack Kennedy always had the courage of his convictions.

Joe, an established campus hero, could be quiet and dignified. Jack had to assert himself in other ways. Usually his hair was disheveled. In the morning he usually pulled on whatever clothes were on top of the heap in his room. The room itself was magnificently untidy, despite his promises to keep it more neatly.

Even a severe case of double pneumonia while he was at Choate did not slow Jack Kennedy down for long. With several close friends he became one of "The Muckers," a name they gave themselves. Exasperated by their pranks and their skirting of the school's regulations, Choate's headmaster called them something else. Before the whole school at chapel he described the pranksters as "public enemies."

This was enough to scare the lighthearted Muckers into some attempt at reform. Jack Kennedy began to study a little harder. He loved history. Languages and science continued to bore him. He still spelled badly and constructed his themes awkwardly, but his English master found talent in his work. He thought that if Jack Kennedy could ever learn to apply himself he might become a writer. Instead, Jack Kennedy applied himself to the Choate yearbook. For two years he was its very successful business manager. He was particularly good at talking businessmen into placing advertisements in it.

"Ken" Kennedy graduated from The Choate School in 1935 when he was 18 years old. Scholastically he was 64th in a class of 112. He was not a varsity athlete. Yet his classmates voted him the man most likely to succeed in later life. Somehow they were aware of qualities in him which neither his grades nor his athletic prowess showed.

Jack Kennedy (second from right), too light to make the regular Choate football team, played on his class team.

He was quick. He had a gift for saying the right thing to the right people at the right time. He was a fighter, and he stuck to his guns. He never quit. His classmates knew he had a capacity for leadership which was not yet fully formed or always apparent to others.

To the surprise and disappointment of his father, Jack Kennedy chose to go not to Harvard, where Joe Jr. was already an undergraduate, but to Princeton. Several of his close friends at Choate were going there. His father accepted his decision, but he had a suggestion. Joe Jr. had studied under the socialist economist, Harold Laski, at the London School of Economics in England. Anxious for his sons to have the best possible education, Joseph P. Kennedy suggested that Jack spend the summer between prep school and college studying under the same liberal thinker.

Joe had told Professor Laski, as he told others, that he intended to be the first Catholic President of the United States. Joe made no secret of his ambition and his plans. If Jack Kennedy thought of the Presidency in those days, it was probably as something belonging to his older brother.

Obediently Jack sailed for England and began his studies, but he did not get far. He developed a jaundice condition and was put into a

We're puttin' on our top hat.

Tyin' up our white tie.

Brushin' off our tails.

In order to
Wish you

A Merry Christmas

Rip.   Leem.   Ken.

As a Princeton freshman in 1935, "Ken" Kennedy, with two of his classmates, sent this Christmas card.

London hospital. As soon as he was well enough to leave, he returned, ill and shaken, skin and eyes yellowed from the disease, for another long summer of slow recovery at Hyannis Port.

From the wide porch of his father's big white house on the knoll overlooking Nantucket Sound he watched the sun shimmering on the waves and listened to the cries of the gulls. He breathed the salt air and the scent of the pines. As he began to improve, he played tennis and golf and, as often as he could, sailed the 25-foot Victura, his racing sloop which had been built at the century-old Crosby yards seven or eight miles away in Osterville. The Victura and the Marlin, the family's big cruiser, were always the first boats in the water at Hyannis Port in the spring and the last to be taken out in the fall.

He was still not too well. His illness delayed his entering Princeton until several weeks after the fall term of 1935 had started. It reoccurred severely and forced him to leave Princeton even before the football season was over. This time his doctors ordered him to Arizona to recuperate in the warm, dry air of the Southwest.

Jack Kennedy had suffered from diphtheria when he was a very small boy. His schooling at Canterbury had been cut short by appendicitis. He had been very ill with pneumonia at Choate. His attendance at the London School of Economics and at Princeton had been ended by jaundice. Illness had plagued him all through his school career, but he seemed much better by the fall of 1936.

Rather than return to Princeton where he would be a year behind his Choate friends and former classmates, he entered Harvard College as a freshman in the class of 1940.

Joe Jr., in the class of 1938, was on the Harvard football squad. An honor student, a member of student council, active in campus politics and a class officer, he was one of the most popular men at Harvard.

Still trying to emulate his older brother, Jack Kennedy went out for end in freshman football and for swimming. He made both frosh teams. As committee chairman for the annual Freshman Smoker, he brought a popular New York singer with a cast of 40 in as the main feature of that gala evening. Jack Kennedy was a graduate of a name preparatory school, the son of a father headlined in the news, the brother of an admired campus figure and a C student. There was little else to distinguish him from his classmates.

As a sophomore he tried out for both football and swimming. When he could not make the Harvard football squad, he played on the junior varsity. In one scrimmage he badly injured his back, dislocating a vertebra. This was the beginning of a physical disability which affected him for the rest of his life.

Jack Kennedy swam the backstroke event for the varsity swimming team when he was a student at Harvard.

John F. Kennedy, who traveled widely, is shown returning in 1938 from a summer in Europe.

He made the swimming squad but failed to make the team which swam against Yale. Most of Jack Kennedy's Harvard athletics came in intramural competition. He played hockey and softball and swam for Winthrop House where he lived.

The high point of Jack Kennedy's sporting career at Harvard came in 1938 when, in Kennedy home waters off Wianno near Hyannis Port, he and a classmate sailed Harvard to victory over nine other Eastern colleges. They won the intercollegiate yachting championship and the coveted MacMillan Cup.

Between freshman and sophomore years he and a friend toured Europe. They went to England, France, Spain and to Italy, where Jack had an audience with the Pope. Late in the fall of his sophomore year his father was appointed Ambassador to Great Britain.

Jack Kennedy was still an undistinguished student, well down in the lower half of his class. He made the editorial board of The Crimson, Harvard's newspaper. A member of St. Paul's Catholic Club all four years, he made the socially correct Spee Club and his father's club, Hasty Pudding. He did not enter into campus politics, debating or any of the student movements which stirred about him as seething Europe drew closer to World War II. In May 1938 Jack became a millionaire in his own right. Joseph P. Kennedy gave each of his children a million-dollar trust when they became 21.

Most of the family now were in England. Ambassador Kennedy was proving a colorful and popular envoy. He was the intimate and the trusted confidant of Prime Minister Neville Chamberlain and of many others in high office in the British Government. The Kennedy family moved now in high international society.

Jack got a leave of absence from Harvard for the second half of his junior year. Early in 1939 he returned to Europe to work part of the time under his father's direction and part of the time under that of William Bullitt, the United States Ambassador to France. Ambassador Kennedy sent both Joe and Jack to troubled spots throughout Europe with orders to report to him on delicate and difficult political situations.

Jack Kennedy was sent to France, Russia, the Balkan States, Palestine, Italy and Germany. He was fascinated by what he saw and heard. He had chosen government as his major study at Harvard and had been reading about it in books. Now in many countries he watched the operations of government at first hand. He began to develop the capacity for acute observation and clear judgment which was to serve him so importantly later. His reports to his father were accurate and of practical value to the American Embassy in London.

One night after he returned from Egypt to the American Embassy in Berlin, the American chargé d'affaires told Jack Kennedy to return immediately to London and tell Ambassador Kennedy that Germany

As a senior at Harvard majoring in government, John Kennedy was vitally interested in world affairs.

. . . The Communists rest everything on the idea of a monolithic world. . . . The pursuit of knowledge, on the other hand, rests everything on the opposite idea—on the idea of a world based on diversity, self-determination, freedom.

University of California, Berkeley, California, March 23, 1962

. . . Leadership and learning are indispensable to each other. The advancement of learning depends on community leadership for financial and political support—and the products of that learning, in turn, are essential to the leadership's hopes for continued progress and prosperity. . . .

To have been delivered at Dallas, Texas, Nov. 22, 1963

. . . It is well to remember that this nation's first great leaders, our founders, Jefferson, Madison, Monroe, . . . Mason, Bryant and all the rest, were not only the political leaders of this country, but they were also among the most educated citizens that this country had ever produced.

Tacoma, Washington, Sept. 27, 1963

planned to march against Poland within a few days. Jack rushed back to London, arriving there just in time to warn his father of the outbreak of World War II which began September 1, 1939.

The day after war was declared Ambassador Kennedy ordered his 22-year-old son to Glasgow, Scotland, to look after the Americans who had survived the sinking of the Athenia. The English liner carrying 1,418 passengers had been torpedoed without warning by a German submarine.

Jack Kennedy was a celebrity at Harvard when he returned for his senior year. He had participated in the opening actions of global conflict. He had been in the midst of world explosion. His college friends looked on him with a certain awe.

Jack Kennedy had changed. What he had seen and experienced had struck home. His mind had been challenged. He was now a vitally interested observer of world affairs. Government and political science came alive for him. The indifferent student of freshman and sophomore years now became a serious student. He even decided to try for honors in political science. That meant that in addition to his regular classroom work he had to write a long serious paper on some problem in government. For his thesis subject he chose a study of the mistakes in foreign policy which had brought England and most of Europe into war.

He called his thesis "Appeasement at Munich." It was not the best honors paper ever submitted at Harvard. In places it was awkward in thought and composition. Yet Jack Kennedy's professors saw that his ideas were important and that his conclusions were sound.

In England, Ambassador Kennedy was proud both of his son's graduating from Harvard College with honors and of his thesis. In long letters to his son he discussed the ideas Jack had put forward. The idea of rewriting and polishing the thesis into a possible book took shape. The Ambassador suggested editorial advisers, literary agents and possible publishers. Jack Kennedy did more research—adding substance to his work—and more writing. On the advice of one of his father's friends on The New York Times, he changed the title to *Why England Slept*. Henry Luce, publisher of Time and Life and another of his father's friends, wrote an introduction for the book. A publisher accepted it, and it was published.

Quickly the small book by the 23-year-old author who had just graduated from college became a national best seller. The war was on in Europe. Germany's well-trained and mechanized armies were sweeping across Europe in an almost unhindered blitzkrieg. The Allies had been unprepared. France had fallen. England just managed to save the remnants of her army at Dunkirk. Under terrible aerial bombardment she was threatened with invasion. The democracies seemed helpless before Adolf Hitler and his Nazi armies.

Jack Kennedy's book was timely and informative. He did not blame the statesmen of England for the war. He blamed the English people themselves for their indifference and apathy despite the obvious danger. He questioned whether the democracies could fight the Fascist countries without themselves becoming totalitarian states. He urged the United States to rearm for war.

Ambassador Kennedy himself was convinced that the democracies could not win. He was under bombardment in England and knew at first hand the power of the enemy and the weaknesses of the Allies. The democracies might not even survive. He thought and said that sending financial and military aid to Great Britain would prove useless, and he urged that the United States stay outside the conflict.

Ambassador Kennedy had been mentioned frequently as a possible Democratic candidate for President in 1940. When President Roosevelt announced that he would run for a precedent-breaking third term, that possibility vanished, and Mr. Kennedy announced that he would support Franklin D. Roosevelt again. When the events of the war proved that his judgments about Great Britain and the other European Allies had been wrong, he resigned his ambassadorship. Joseph P. Kennedy never again held public office. Like his father before him, he worked quietly but effectively behind the political scene.

Wide World

JOHN FITZGERALD KENNEDY

Born May 29, 1917, in Brookline, Massachusetts. Prepared at The Choate School. Home Address: 294 Pondfield Road, Bronxville, New York. Winthrop House. *Crimson* (2–4); Chairman Smoker Committee (1); St. Paul's Catholic Club (1–4). Football (1), Junior Varsity (2); Swimming (1), Squad (2). Golf (1). House Hockey (3, 4); House Swimming (2); House Softball (4). Hasty Pudding-Institute of 1770; Spee Club. Permanent Class Committee. Field of Concentration: Government. Intended Vocation: Law.

In the yearbook for the Harvard class of 1940, John F. Kennedy listed his intended vocation as law.

Ens. John F. Kennedy speaks with a group of Naval recruits in South Carolina in 1942.

After his duty in the Pacific, "Shafty" Kennedy found time to relax as a PT boat instructor in Miami.

LIEUTENANT JOHN F. (SHAFTY) KENNEDY, USNR

In the Harvard class album for the class of 1940 Jack Kennedy had listed law as his preferred vocation. Joe Jr. was in the Harvard Law School. Jack decided he would enter Yale Law. Then he changed his mind and went instead to Stanford University in California where for six months he studied business courses. Restlessly, he gave this up and took a long trip through South America.

The war in Europe was being bitterly fought. It looked as if the Allies were almost certain to lose. It looked too as if the United States might be drawn into the conflict at any moment. It was difficult for a young man to know what to do.

Joe Jr. decided first. He had already started his political career by serving as a delegate at the Democratic National Convention which that year renominated Franklin D. Roosevelt for the Presidency. Joe left Harvard and became a Naval Aviation cadet.

Jack Kennedy then tried to get into the Army. He could not pass the physical examination. He tried the Navy next. Again he was rejected because of his injured back. Refusal only made him the more determined to get into the service. At Hyannis Port he began to do a series of strenuous physical exercises to strengthen his back. He kept them up for months. When he felt certain that he could pass, he applied again to the Navy. This time he got through his physical successfully and won a direct commission in the Naval Reserve.

John F. Kennedy is shown at the wheel of PT 109 which was struck and sunk by a destroyer on August 2, 1943.

His first assignment in uniform was to help prepare a new digest for Naval Intelligence in Washington. He spent more than a year in Washington and as a Naval officer at defense plants in the South. In December 1941, immediately after Japan bombed Pearl Harbor without warning and the United States was officially at war with Germany and Japan, he applied for combat duty. Late in 1942 he was sent to motor torpedo boat training schools in Portsmouth, New Hampshire, and in Rhode Island.

Early in 1943 he was shipped out of San Francisco to a PT base at Rendova in the Solomon Islands in the South Pacific. There he was placed in command of PT 109 with a crew of 10 men and 2 other officers. The 109 was part of a squadron of PT boats operating near Guadalcanal Island in the Solomon Islands.

Behind his father's house in Hyannis Port was another big white house which years later Jack Kennedy purchased. In it lived an older man who had taught him much of what he knew of the sea and seamanship. The new skipper sent his friend a photograph of himself stripped to the waist in the South Pacific heat, a Navy fatigue cap on his head. Across the bottom he wrote, "Look what you got me into!"

Jack Kennedy had been handling small boats since childhood. He had been sailing with or against Joe at Hyannis Port ever since he could remember. He handled his 80-foot plywood craft with its three engines like the Cape Codder he was. The PT boats carried four small torpedoes, mounted one 20-mm. cannon and four .50-caliber machine guns. They were doing much damage in the American sea and air island-to-island counterattack against Japan.

PT 109 carried out 30 attack and strafing missions against Japanese ships and shore installations with no casualties and without being seriously damaged. At 2 A.M. on August 2, 1943, she was the lead ship of three American PT boats patrolling in search of an enemy target. The night was black. The 109 was running on one engine to keep down the noise. "Shafty" Kennedy, as his mates called the lean, 6-foot one-inch skipper, was at the wheel. Ens. George Ross from Princeton was on the bow straining with binoculars to see ahead.

Suddenly a towering shape rose above them. Out of the night a Japanese destroyer bore down at 30 knots. She struck the 109 amidships, knifing it in two, and the PT boat exploded in flames. Jack Kennedy and his radioman were hurled to the deck. The stern half of the boat sank as high-octane gasoline flared blindingly over the black waters. The front half to which Kennedy and four others clung was kept afloat by its watertight compartments. The Japanese destroyer scarcely slowed. Assuming that the 109 had been lost with all hands, the other PT boats continued on course and disappeared into the night.

Flashing a light, the skipper called out. Ensign Ross and five others were swimming close at hand. The 109's engineer, Machinist's Mate Patrick McMahon, had been badly burned. Another of the crew had an injured leg. Kennedy dived into the water and towed them to the still floating half of what had been his command.

Two men, either killed in the explosion or drowned, were never found. Eleven of the 13 aboard were accounted for. All night they clung to the half hulk hoping to be rescued. The next day, when it turned over in the water and they knew it would soon sink, they decided to swim to a small island 3½ miles away. Closer islands were held by the Japanese.

Jack Kennedy's back had been reinjured when he was slammed to the deck, but there was no time to worry about that now. He was an expert swimmer. McMahon's legs were so badly burned that he could not swim. Kennedy took the strap of the engineer's life belt between his teeth and set off with a breast-stroke towing the injured man. The salt water poured in through his clenched teeth. Every few minutes he had to stop to rest. It took them four hours to make that 3½ miles, but all of the remaining crew made it to the island.

The small island had few palm trees but was covered with tall casuarina trees. After a brief rest, Shafty Kennedy swam about two or three miles to Ferguson Passage where the American PT boats slipped down from their base to the open sea. All that night, swimming and treading water, he held up a heavy ship's lantern to signal any rescue boat. None came.

While he was seeking help, a shower had drenched the island and the thirsty men had licked the leaves of the shrubs. They found the rain water to be bitter, and in the morning discovered the leaves were white with bird droppings. For this reason they named the place Bird Island.

At dawn Kennedy made his way to a tiny nearby island where he fell into a deep sleep. Late that morning, he returned to his men and collapsed exhausted. That night he sent Ross to repeat his attempt. Again no boats came through the Passage. PT 109 had been reported lost. A memorial service had been held at Rendova.

The following day, Shafty Kennedy decided to move his men to Olasana, an island nearer the Passage. Strap between his teeth again, he towed the badly burned but uncomplaining McMahon for the three hours it took them to reach the neighboring island.

Bird Island had provided little food, but Olasana abounded in coconut trees. Breaking the coconuts open the exhausted men drank the milk and ate the meat but it made them ill.

The next day luck was with Kennedy and Ross when they decided to swim to Nauru, another island about a half mile away and closer to Ferguson Passage. They spotted the wreckage of a small Japanese ship on the reef and, near to it, a rope-bound crate of hard candy. Exploring further, they came across a native dugout canoe and a large tin of rain water. At that moment they spotted two figures aboard the Japanese wreck. Each pair fled in terror fearing that the other was Japanese. The men on the wreckage—who turned out to be native scouts—paddled their canoe to Olasana where they came upon Kennedy's men.

After a long wait in the bushes on Nauru, Shafty Kennedy piled the candy and water into the canoe and, using slats from the crate for paddles, rowed back to Olasana leaving Ross on the island.

After giving the supplies to the men, Kennedy paddled back, picked up Ross and started for Ferguson Passage. A sudden squall overturned the small craft and the men and canoe were hurled against the coral reef at Nauru. Ross was badly cut up.

The next morning Kennedy and Ross returned to Olasana. Feeling that he had to have faith in the natives, who were staying in his camp,

Kennedy scratched a message on a coconut shell and entrusted it to them:

NATIVE KNOWS POSIT
HE CAN PILOT 11 ALIVE NEED SMALL BOAT
KENNEDY

The following day Kennedy received a message from an Australian coastwatcher stationed just off New Georgia:

To Senior Officer, Nauru Is.
Friday 11 P.M. Have just learnt of your presence on Nauru Is. & also that two natives have taken news to Rendova. I strongly advise you return immediately to here in this canoe & by the time you arrive here I will be in radio communication with authorities at Rendova & we can finalise plans to collect balance your party. Will warn aviation of your crossing Ferguson Passage.

A. R. Evans, Lt.
R.A.N.V.R.
(Royal Australian Naval
Village Reserve)

The seven natives who arrived with the message brought a canoe filled with food—yams, pawpaws, rice, potatoes, boiled fish, C rations.

After the men had eaten, the messengers hid Shafty Kennedy under palm fronds in the bottom of their canoe and paddled him back to meet Evans. That night a PT boat picked up Kennedy and he guided it back to get the other survivors of PT 109.

"For heroism in the rescue of three men following the ramming and sinking of his motor torpedo boat. . ." Lieut. (jg.) John F. Kennedy was decorated with the Navy and Marine Corps Medal. He was also awarded the Purple Heart.

As is customary, the rescued men were ordered back to the United States, but Shafty Kennedy asked for, and got, a second tour of duty in PT boats in the South Pacific. He suffered from his reinjured back. He contracted malaria. When he did return to the United States, it was a very happy but very thin young officer who reported for duty as a PT boat instructor at Miami. Miami offered recreations not available on Bird Island, and he was able to spend weekends at the Kennedy family home in Palm Beach.

In the spring of 1944 Lieutenant Kennedy was forced to enter the hospital for a disk operation on his spine. The aftermath was long and painful. He was on a weekend leave from the hospital at Hyannis Port, in August 1944 when news came that Joe Jr. was missing in action.

His own flying tour completed, Joe had volunteered to pilot a plane loaded with high explosives against a German rocket base on the coast of Belgium. The plane was to act as a bomb after its pilot and co-pilot had bailed out. Instead it exploded in mid-air. The bodies of the two men

Lieut. John Kennedy is congratulated by Capt. Frederick L. Conklin after being awarded the Navy and Marine Corps Medal for heroism.

were never found.

The closely welded Kennedy family was grief-stricken. The father who had lost his first-born was inconsolable. Joe had been the leader, the vital, forceful hero of all his brothers and sisters, the Kennedy who expected so much of himself—even the Presidency—and of whom they all had expected so much.

Jack Kennedy was numbed. Joe had been his ideal. Joe and he had fought battle after battle, but usually because he was trying to be as big and as strong as Joe.

Another blow followed. Jack's favorite sister, Kathleen, had married the Marquess of Huntington, heir of the Duke of Devonshire. A captain in the Coldstream Guards, he was killed in action four months after the marriage. Jack grieved for his sister's grief. Three years later Kathleen was killed in the crash of a private plane over France.

During his long stay at Chelsea, Jack Kennedy wrote his second book. It was not a best seller. It was not meant to be. It was a privately printed memorial volume, *As We Remember Joe*, to which the family and a few of Joe's closest friends contributed 20 essays. Illustrated with many pictures of Joe in college, abroad and in the Navy, it was issued from the University Press in Cambridge in 1945 and copies were distributed to the family and to Joe's friends.

Early in 1945, Lieut. John F. Kennedy received a medical discharge from the United States Navy.

THE HONORABLE JOHN F. KENNEDY, U.S. HOUSE OF REPRESENTATIVES

Joe who someday would have probably run for President was dead. Robert, nine years younger than Jack, served as an enlisted man aboard the U.S.S. Joseph P. Kennedy Jr., a destroyer named in memory of their brother. It was up to John Fitzgerald Kennedy, the next in line, to take over. Perhaps he could ease the loss to his father and mother. His father wished him to take over.

Yet there was more to it than that. When he was able to walk without crutches, then without a stick, Jack Kennedy worked for a few months as a reporter for Hearst's International News Service. He covered the charter meeting of the United Nations and the English elections of 1946.

This job did not satisfy him. He was a writer but a thoughtful observer rather than a factual reporter. As an aide to his father before the war he had been on the inside. Now he was outside, and there was a difference. He was 28 years old. Like millions of other young men, he had lost years from any possible career while in the armed forces. He could be a college teacher, but that would take several years of graduate schooling, and he felt he had no more time to lose.

Jack Kennedy had been bred in the atmosphere of politics. He had emerged from Harvard a skilled observer of politics on an international scale. In the Navy he had proved, most importantly to himself, that he had a capacity for leadership, and he saw politics in terms of leaders. Politics was the family profession, and he felt equipped for it. This Jack Kennedy had a self-confidence that only a few years before he had lacked.

The fabled James M. Curley, long-time mayor of Boston and Governor of Massachusetts was serving in Congress. He now decided to run for mayor again rather than for re-election to the House. Thus the Democratic nomination for Representative from the 11th Massachusetts Congressional District was open.

The 11th was a district of Irish and Italian immigrants, of tenements, factories and freight yards and had once been largely controlled by Jack

John F. Kennedy began his political career in 1946 when he filed nomination papers to run for the House of Representatives.

Kennedy's grandfather Patrick J. Kennedy. It was also the district of Harvard University across the Charles in Cambridge. As the 11th always went Democratic, the main problem for Jack Kennedy was the nomination. He declared himself a candidate and went to work.

Every one of the Kennedys gave full support to him. Friends from Choate, Harvard and the Navy came at his call and pitched in. Thin, looking much younger than he was, unmistakably the product of a select preparatory school and Harvard, Jack Kennedy was not at all the kind of politician people in the district were accustomed to.

He was hesitant at first, unsure of himself. He did not speak easily from the platform. He had to overcome an initial distaste for the hand-shaking, the backslapping, the deals. He had to learn the methods of self-advertisement which the officeseeker must use. Just because it was distasteful, Jack Kennedy went at it hard. He wanted to win, and he had always wanted to be liked and tried to make people like him.

He shook hands. He talked on street corners. He went into saloons, barbershops, stores, factories and fire stations and shook hands and asked men and women for their votes. He visited people in their homes, shook hands and talked about rent control, jobs, social security, medical care for the aged. He promised that if he were nominated and then elected he would do all he could to improve living and working conditions for them. Then he shook hands again and left.

His hard-working assistants staged house parties all over the district, sometimes five or six in an evening. Jack showed up at all of them. Honey Fitz swung joyously into the campaign, enlisting hardened ward politicians to help out his grandson's amateur enthusiasts. Following the campaign closely from Hyannis Port, Joseph P. Kennedy hired a skilled and experienced manager to head his son's staff.

Jack Kennedy's electioneering improved with practice. As his chances of winning the nomination grew, his spirits rose. In the United States a man has to be a politician before he can be a statesman. If Jack Kennedy had had any doubts about that, they vanished in his first campaign. So did his qualms about practical politics. Politics was a more

We are politicians in the sense that we believe political action through one of the political parties . . . is the best means of achieving service for our country. . . . These matters do not end on election day. All this is a means to an end, not an end in itself, and the end is service to our country. . . .

Jefferson-Jackson Day Brunch,
Middletown, Ohio, Oct. 17, 1960

complicated game than football, with trickier plays. It demanded mental and emotional skills. The young man who many at Harvard had thought shy and something of a loner became an artist in persuading people.

There was a great final party in a Cambridge hotel. By invitation some 2,000 women voters came to meet Ambassador and Mrs. Rose Fitzgerald Kennedy and the candidate's pretty sisters.

On the day of the primary election, John F. Kennedy voted early with his Fitzgerald grandparents. Then he disappeared alone into a movie house and watched *A Night in Casablanca*. He won the nomination with more than twice as many votes as his nearest rival. That fall he was elected to the United States House of Representatives.

John Kennedy was 29 years old when he took his seat in Congress. In appearance he might still have been a Harvard undergraduate, but he was a combat veteran who had proved himself a vote-getting politician. In college and in Europe he had been an entranced observer of government. He had ceased now to be only an observer. He was a responsible and active participant in the Government of the United States. It was what he wished. His life in national public office and in national public service had begun.

The freshman Representative was nobody's man. He owed his seat to no political boss, not even to his own party. With the aid of his father, his family and loyal friends of his own age and background, he had won it for himself. He could be independent, and he was.

Continually devouring newspapers, magazines and books, he knew where to find the facts about any question quickly and fully. On the basis of the facts he made up his mind, reached his decisions and voted for or against proposed measures.

He believed that low-cost public housing was needed. He spoke for it and voted for it, even fighting powerful veterans' organizations which opposed it. He fought for labor, opposing the Taft-Hartley Act which limited the powers of the labor unions.

He knew the excitement of being in Washington and in Congress, but, like other new young Representatives, he felt disillusionment and some frustration. Legislative power lay with the older men of long experience who sat on important committees. Government moves slowly, and Jack Kennedy was eager and impatient.

This was the Democratic Administration of President Harry S. Truman. Instead of blindly supporting all of its policies, Kennedy attacked the Administration for its foreign policy and for its program of cuts in defense spending.

After he had been in Congress for several years the question arose of sending American military forces to help protect Western Europe against Communism. Congressman Kennedy visited England, France, Italy, Spain, Yugoslavia and West Germany to see conditions for himself. On

White House Photo: Abbie Rowe

Mothers may want their sons to grow up to be President, Mr. Kennedy said, but they do not want them to become politicians in the process.

his return he was invited to speak before a joint meeting of the Senate's Foreign Relations and Armed Services committees. He told the Senators that he favored sending American forces abroad, but that he thought the Western European countries should provide more forces of their own.

A bachelor, John Kennedy lived in a house in Georgetown, an old but fashionable section of Washington along the Potomac, where he had a housekeeper and a valet. When he had a chance, he pulled on an old pair of Navy chinos, took a baseball glove or a football and played with the boys in a Georgetown playground. Most of the boys had no idea that the skinny new guy in the game was a Congressman.

He went out often on dates. He went often to the movies, usually to Westerns, which he liked best. He dined out frequently. He traveled widely. He took many weekend trips to keep in touch with people in his district. He flew to Palm Beach or Hyannis Port. He took quick trips abroad. In 1951 with a brother and sister he went around the world.

If he wishes to remain in office, a Congressman must be re-elected every two years. Every two years he must stage a new campaign. Actually, through letters, speeches and meetings, most Congressmen are campaigning all the time. Congressman Kennedy did not have to campaign much. The 11th Massachusetts always went Democratic. In 1948 he had no opponent for the nomination, and no Republican ran against him in the fall election. In 1950 he beat his Republican opponent by the reassuring margin of five votes to one.

Though there seemed little need, Congressman Kennedy campaigned anyway. He thrived on competition. At every opportunity he visited cities and towns outside his district. He made speeches. He shook hands. With an ex-prizefighter chauffeur and his campaign manager he drove to veterans' meetings, flower shows, women's clubs, factories— anywhere in Massachusetts where he could be seen and heard.

In 1950 he returned to The Choate School to speak at its 50th anniversary. He urged that Choate instill in its students an interest in politics and the national life. He deplored the contempt in which too many educated Americans hold politics. He asked that the privileged graduates of Choate and other private schools assume their due share of responsibility for public service.

Earnestly he quoted the Swiss-born writer Jean Jacques Rousseau: "As soon as any man says of the affairs of the State, 'What does it matter to me?' the State may be given up for lost."

Though he quoted Rousseau this time, John Kennedy was more apt to quote an Irish-born English statesman of the 18th century. It was his favorite quotation, and he had taken the words of Edmund Burke to heart: "The only thing necessary for the triumph of evil is for good men to do nothing."

In 1952, after he had served three terms in the House of Representatives, John F. Kennedy announced that he would run for the United States Senate against Henry Cabot Lodge.

Senator Lodge had held the seat since 1936. A liberal Republican, like Kennedy a Harvard graduate, he had seen combat service with the Army in North Africa and Europe during World War II. He was popular, respected and the chief supporter of General Dwight D. Eisenhower for the Republican nomination for President. His grandfather, the first Henry Cabot Lodge, had defeated Kennedy's grandfather Honey Fitz for this same Senate seat. Expert political opinion was that young Jack Kennedy did not have a chance.

THE HONORABLE JOHN F. KENNEDY, SENATOR FROM MASSACHUSETTS

Kennedy money, Kennedy influence, Kennedy backing were poured into this fight. The Congressman's younger brother Robert was made fighting campaign manager. The candidate's sisters left their own jobs and interests in various parts of the country to work without letup at the Kennedy campaign headquarters in Boston. Joseph P. Kennedy came from behind the scenes to appear for his son. Rose Fitzgerald Kennedy proved one of her son's most appealing and effective advocates. She appeared both on the speaker's platform and at formal receptions for women voters which members of the Kennedy family staged in place after place in Massachusetts.

Public relations experts were hired. Advertising experts were hired. Radio and television were used. Placards blazoned the Kennedy name. Massachusetts rang with it. The Choate, Harvard and Navy volunteers who had worked hard for Jack Kennedy before worked twice as hard now. Jack Kennedy charmed and persuaded. Robert Kennedy drove his amateur and professional staff at a faster and faster pace. The Kennedys believed in winning, and they wanted bitterly to win this one. They were out to win. They fought to win, and they did win.

Dwight D. Eisenhower defeated Adlai Stevenson for President by a huge majority, Massachusetts going Republican for the first time in many years. In the same election, Democrat John F. Kennedy defeated Republican Henry Cabot Lodge, grandson of his family's old political enemy, by 70,000 votes.

Escorted by Leverett Saltonstall, the senior Senator from Massachusetts, John Fitzgerald Kennedy took the oath of office and his Senate seat January 3, 1953.

Robert Kennedy (left) served as campaign manager for his brother throughout his political career.

Senator Kennedy espoused the same liberal causes which Congressman Kennedy had supported. He spoke and voted for public housing, minimum-wage laws and the protection, maintenance and expansion of the country's natural resources in land and water. As a Senator he could speak now for an entire state and, because that state was Massachusetts, for an entire area. His chief stand in the Senate during his first six-year term was for measures that would improve economic conditions in declining New England.

In his crowded and busy Senate office and in the offices he maintained in Boston, Senator Kennedy worked hard for his constituents. He answered their questions, helped them with business problems involving the Federal Government, and performed the thousand and one favors Senators are expected to perform for those whose votes will keep them in office. Surrounded by a zealous staff of legal, publicity and clerical assistants, he did these things more quickly and more efficiently than most Senators and Congressmen. Both on the Senate floor and in his offices the 36-year-old Senator strove to live up to his campaign promise to "do more for Massachusetts."

We shall be judged more by what we do at home than by what we preach abroad. . . . These domestic tasks do not divert our energy or our security—they provide the very foundation for freedom's survival and success.

State of the Union Address to Congress,
Washington, D.C., Jan. 14, 1963

I hope, in other words, that we will take this rich country of ours, given to us by God and by nature, and improve it through science and find new uses for our natural resources. . . .

Great Falls, Montana, Sept. 26, 1963

Our national conservation effort must include the complete spectrum of resources: air, water and land; fuels, energy and minerals; soils, forests and forage; fish and wildlife. Together they make up the world of nature which surrounds us—a vital part of the American heritage.

Message to Congress, Washington, D.C., March 1, 1962

Senator Kennedy often found time to stroll along the beach at Hyannis Port with his nephews, Bobby Shriver (left) and Bobby Kennedy Jr.

Jack and Jacqueline Kennedy pose with their wedding party after their marriage in Newport, Rhode Island, in 1953.

On September 12, 1953, at the Newport, Rhode Island estate of her wealthy and socially prominent family, Senator John F. Kennedy married Jacqueline Lee Bouvier, a tall, dark-haired young woman of unusual grace and beauty and a student of the arts. Robert Kennedy was best man at the wedding which was attended by some 1,200 guests. Richard Cardinal Cushing, then Archbishop of the archdiocese of Boston, performed the ceremony and read a special blessing from the Pope. It was the social event of the Newport season. Police were unable to hold back an enthralled crowd of some 3,000 spectators.

Senator Kennedy had purchased the big white house in Hyannis Port diagonally behind the home of his father and that of his brother Robert, the three homes making the "Kennedy Compound." He now bought a showplace home in Virginia, "Hickory Hill," which had been the headquarters of General George McClellan during the Civil War, but the newly married couple had hardly got under way with their new life when John Kennedy fell victim to an old disability.

The furious pace he had kept up in his campaigning and in Congress

In his busy schedule as a Senator, John F. Kennedy found time to sign autographs for a group of Girl Scouts who visited his office.

had aggravated his back injury. For some time he had been forced to wear a sort of light corset for support. He had sometimes had to use a cane. As the pain—about which he never complained—grew worse, he was forced back on crutches.

On October 21, 1954, Senator Kennedy went into a New York hospital for a double fusion of disks in his spine, a delicate and dangerous operation. For weeks afterward he lay on his back in a darkened room. He had to be given frequent blood transfusions.

He did not recover quickly or easily. At Christmas he was flown on a stretcher in the plane to Palm Beach for the holidays at home with his family. By January they all knew that another operation would be necessary. It was performed in New York in mid-February. Before the end of the month he was able to walk, with assistance, from the hospital.

A long convalescence in Florida followed. Jack Kennedy could sleep only a little while at a time. Often he was in intense pain. In bed or, when he was able, sitting in sunlight by the Kennedy swimming pool he continued work on a new book he had begun to write in the hospital.

Its subject had been in his mind for years. Aides in Washington did much of the preliminary research. The Library of Congress sent him parcels of books. Professors and lawyers helped with advice but the ideas were Kennedy's. So was the actual writing of *Profiles in Courage*.

The courage which Jack Kennedy celebrated in this book was not the kind of courage he had shown all his life. It was the political courage shown by United States Congressmen who had fought for causes in which they believed despite the opposition of their constituents and often with the full knowledge that what they were doing might well mean the end of their political careers.

John Quincy Adams, Sam Houston, Daniel Webster, George Norris, Edmund Ross, Thomas Hart Benton, Lucius Lamar and Robert A. Taft were the Senatorial heroes about whom John Kennedy wrote. He did not mention it, but he had shown the same kind of political heroism himself when, believing it was in the best interests of the country, he spoke and acted in favor of the St. Lawrence Seaway. Many people in Massachusetts were strongly against it. They feared that if ocean-going ships could reach the American Middle West by this system of rivers, lakes and canals, Boston would suffer as a seaport.

When, after his enforced absence of many months, John Kennedy

---

. . . I think, of course, great times make great Presidents and great men. . . . A sense of the future and the past and a wide cultural experience which makes it possible for them to draw on the lives of other men and the experiences of other men and apply it to a particular situation, moral courage, a sense of the future, a sense of the past, a physical vitality, intellectual vitality, intellectual curiosity and purpose. I would say those are the qualities.

Television-Radio Debate, Chicago, Illinois, Sept. 26, 1960

It is in times such as these that many men, weak in courage and frail in nerve, develop the tendency to turn suspiciously on their neighbors and leaders. Unable to face up to the dangers from without, they become convinced that the real danger is from within.

Washington, D.C., June 22, 1962

Members of the Congress, the Constitution makes us not rivals for power but partners for progress. We are all trustees for the American people, custodians of the American heritage. It is my task to *report* the state of the Union—to *improve* it is the task of us all.

State of the Union Address to Congress,
Washington, D.C., Jan. 11, 1962

returned to the Senate, his fellows rose in a body and applauded. Lyndon Johnson as Democratic Leader and William Knowland as Republican Leader greeted him officially. Among the many messages and gifts piled high in his office was a welcome-home present from his friend Vice President Richard Nixon.

That fall a woman doctor in New York gave John Kennedy the first substantial and lasting relief from pain since his operations by injecting large amounts of Novocain which relieved the muscle spasms in his back. In January 1956, *Profiles in Courage*, dedicated to his wife, was published. It was another best seller, and this time John F. Kennedy received the coveted Pulitzer Prize for biography.

In the Senate he began to make up for lost time. He did this so well, and his political forces were so well organized that he was one of the most prominent members of his party when the Democratic National Convention assembled in Chicago in 1956. He delivered the speech renominating Adlai Stevenson for President, and Stevenson was renominated. Kennedy just missed obtaining the Vice-Presidential nomination himself. It went instead to Senator Estes Kefauver.

A major figure now in national Democratic politics, Senator Kennedy was in great demand this campaign year. After a brief vacation

President Kennedy shares a laugh with former Senate colleagues, (l. to r.) George Smathers, Stuart Symington, Kenneth Keating and Daniel Inouye.

Senator Kennedy adjusts the sail of his boat as Jacqueline watches.

in France, which was interrupted by the serious illness of his wife and the loss of their unborn child, he traveled widely and spoke often in support of the Stevenson-Kefauver ticket. In one five-week period of the campaign he traveled 30,000 miles and made 150 speeches in 26 states. John Kennedy was working for his party's candidates, but he was also making the Kennedy name, the Kennedy smile, the Kennedy charm, the Kennedy courage known across the United States.

It was a relief to relax at Hyannis Port. The thin, untidy boy was now a youthful-appearing man fastidious about his personal appearance, but at home on the Cape he still loved to wear old sports clothes. One evening the Senator invited a number of friends to his father's home to see the first running of a new motion picture musical comedy. He greeted his guests wearing a very old tweed sport jacket.

The show over, he saw some of his guests to the door, then rejoined the others in the long living room. Suddenly he began to jerk, wriggle and twist, and a large moth flew out of the old coat. The undeniable antiquity of his jacket weakened his honest explanation that one of the hundreds of moths attracted by the porch lights had taken refuge in his coat while he was at the door.

In 1958, after another fighting campaign, John F. Kennedy was returned to the Senate by the largest majority won by any Senatorial candidate that year. He had become one of the best-known figures in either

Jack and Jacqueline Kennedy relax together after a game of tennis.

political party, and he knew it. All the Kennedys knew it. His well-trained and experienced political organization knew it. There was no doubt in any of their minds what Jack should try for next. Their every move from 1956 on was calculated toward this end.

Jack Kennedy's growth as man and politician beginning in 1956 amazed even those who were close to him. He had sensed the public's favorable response, and he reacted to it. Always—in Harvard, in the Navy, in his first campaign for Congress—he had responded to challenge. He needed always to have his highest powers challenged to bring out the ability that was in him. It was so now.

He believed deeply in the importance of public life. As he said, in the United States every citizen holds public office. At the same time he became more and more convinced of his own fitness to hold high office, even the highest office. Any uncertainties he may have felt as a boy and a young man disappeared. His weapons were youth, money, intelligence and steadfast purpose. He had seen what he could do with them. He was certain he could do more.

His vigor and freshness were real. They were apparent as, hatless, often without an outer coat even in cold weather, he strode upon a platform or moved quickly forward to greet a visitor. If his back pained, as so often it did, he ignored the pain. The onlooker saw only the handsome Irish face, the sure movements, the youthful spirit. They were part of the man, but he also knew that they were a political asset, and he used them consciously.

MR. PRESIDENT

Late in October 1959, a group of determined men met in Robert Kennedy's house facing the sea in Hyannis Port. There were 17 of them including Joseph P. Kennedy, John, Robert, key men on the Kennedy staff, a public opinion expert, a press relations man, a city machine politician and male Kennedy in-laws.

Senator Kennedy briefed them all in a long session. He listed the political leaders and groups across the country whose support they would have to enlist. He went into detailed accounts of state and local politics in places far distant from Boston or Washington. He had taken careful mental note of many things on his speech-making travels.

Once again Robert Kennedy was made campaign manager. That afternoon each of the others was given his specific assignment. The outlines of a political strategy that was to operate with machinelike precision were laid down. The meeting was serious to the point of grimness.

On January 2, 1960, Senator John F. Kennedy announced that he was a candidate for the Democratic nomination for President.

The first move toward obtaining it was to win the primary elections. In these elections voters of a given party in the various states choose delegates to attend the national convention. These delegates are usually pledged to vote for the candidate winning the primary.

After long and careful preparation the Kennedy forces moved into Wisconsin. The Kennedy professionals and the volunteers went at their assigned tasks. Placards were posted, handbills distributed. Radio and television appeals were put on the air. Senator Kennedy, flying in his own big private plane, visited every town in every important district in the state. He appealed for votes in factories and in clubs, even talked to schoolchildren in their classrooms. He stopped and talked with men and women on the street. Everything went according to precise plan, but Kennedy beat his principal opponent, Senator Hubert Humphrey of Minnesota, by only a small and indecisive margin.

West Virginia came next. More Kennedy supporters and college, Navy and family friends joined the command. The Kennedy professionals moved in on political bosses throughout the state. Press and television poured on the pressure. A motion picture exploited Jack Kennedy's heroism in the South Pacific, showed him receiving the Pulitzer Prize, showed him with his wife and infant daughter, Caroline.

President Kennedy's wit and easy humor were often apparent in his speeches and press conferences.

Kennedy swept the West Virginia primary. He took the Democratic primaries in Indiana, Nebraska, Maryland and Oregon. John F. Kennedy flew up and down around and across the rest of the country, speaking, shaking hands, charming and persuading everywhere. Every Democratic leader of any stature in every region, state and community was approached by the Kennedy organization.

More than 4,500 delegates attended the Democratic National Convention in Los Angeles in 1960. Working with cool efficiency, then with feverish energy, the Kennedy operatives exerted every pressure, wooed with every persuasion. Senators Hubert Humphrey, Stuart Symington and Lyndon Johnson were formidable opponents. Adlai Stevenson was still the favorite of many delegations. But John F. Kennedy beat them all. He won the nomination and selected Lyndon Johnson, who had received the second highest number of votes, as his running mate.

John Fitzgerald Kennedy was a Roman Catholic, and the United States had never elected a Catholic to the Presidency. He was 43 years old, younger than any man ever elected President. The Republicans were in office, and President Eisenhower was an admired and respected

... There isn't any doubt that the center of action in the American constitutional system is the President of the United States. The Constitution places the greatest responsibility for the conduct of our foreign affairs, particularly, upon the President, and unless the President of the United States speaks for the nation, unless the President of the United States is able to personify the force of the nation, then the nation does not move ahead, does not move to accomplish its unfinished business, does not give an image of vitality and strength throughout the world.

Philadelphia, Pennsylvania, Oct. 29, 1960

The other point is something that President Eisenhower said to me on January 19th. He said, "There are no easy matters that will ever come to you as President. If they are easy, they will be settled at a lower level."

Television-Radio Interview: "After Two Years—A Conversation with the President," Washington, D.C., Dec. 17, 1962

I know few significant questions of public policy which can safely be confided to computers. In the end, the hard decisions inescapably involve imponderables of intuition, prudence and judgment.

National Academy of Sciences, Washington, D.C., Oct. 22, 1963

An enthusiastic campaigner, Jack Kennedy was well-informed and handsome, and he had a sure stage presence.

world figure. Richard Nixon, whom the Republicans had nominated, had served for eight years as the country's Vice President. His name was well known. He seemed to have the edge.

The campaign was tense from the start. The pressures were unrelenting. Jack Kennedy spared neither mind nor body in this all-out fight for the office he wanted more than anything else in the world. Neither did his zealous family nor the devoted young men and women who worked for him spare themselves.

California, Maine, Alaska, Michigan, Georgia, Illinois, Arizona—Jack Kennedy appeared everywhere before large and increasingly enthusiastic throngs.

He seemed tireless. He could fly all night in his plane for one appearance, fly half the day for another that night, then all night again for a third speech hundreds of miles away and still appear fresh and vigorous. He knew how to pace himself. Trained from boyhood to compete and compete hard, he could relax although under tension. When a night's rest was impossible, he grabbed bits of sleep on his plane or in a hotel room or at an airport. When he could, he ate his favorite hearty breakfast with two eggs, bacon, toast and milk. When there was no time for meals, he drank soup on the plane. He liked soup, especially cream of tomato soup, but he liked clam chowder best of all. He could and did down five or six bowls of Cape Cod chowder at a sitting and enjoyed the last bowl as much as the first.

When the two candidates for President confronted each other in debate over nationwide television, they reached into the homes of most of the people in the country. Both were young, both personable. Both were professionals experienced in politics and government. On the screen the well-briefed John Kennedy appeared handsome, engaging, well informed and skillful. He had sure stage presence. Always quick on his feet, he was ready, at ease and charming. He had the advantage

U.P.I.

Although John Kennedy campaigned long and strenuously, he appeared tireless.

I f a Negro baby is born—and this is true also of Puerto Ricans and Mexicans in some of our cities—he has about one half as much chance to get through high school as a white baby. He has one third as much chance to get through college as a white student. He has about a third as much chance to be a professional man, and about half as much chance to own a house. He has about four times as much chance that he'll be out of work in his life as the white baby. I think we can do better.

Television-Radio Debate, Chicago, Illinois, Sept. 26, 1960

Mr. Kennedy loved children and found resting at Hyannis Port with his daughter, Caroline, to be the best relaxation.

Three members of a vigorous family, Ted, Robert and Mrs. Ted Kennedy, play touch football on the beach.

of the offense. Richard Nixon, of course, defended the eight years of the Republican Administration.

The debates, four of them beginning with the first in Chicago on September 26, 1960, projected the Kennedy image and personality more successfully than anything else could have done. Obviously, Senator John F. Kennedy was an astute young politician with Presidential ambitions. Just as clearly, he was a vibrantly handsome, highly intelligent young man whose appearance and manner exemplified much that is most admired in a young American.

His appeal was emotional as well as logical. Women reacted to him with enthusiasm. The Roman Catholic vote in the big cities of the North was solidly behind him. Negro votes were won when the Democratic candidate telephoned the wife of a Negro spokesman who had been jailed, offered his sympathy and promised, if necessary, to intervene on her husband's behalf.

Enthusiasm for Kennedy rose in other quarters, particularly in academic and intellectual circles. Many conservatives, like some on the Choate faculty, voted Democratic for the first time in their lives.

Election day was November 8, 1960. Kennedy, his family and his lieutenants, all of them tired from the long campaign, awaited the results at Hyannis Port, where it had all started. The next morning, with the rest of the country, they knew.

He had won, just barely, but he had won. He had received only 112,000 more votes than Richard Nixon, but these were enough to make John Fitzgerald Kennedy the 35th President of the United States.

Jack Kennedy played touch football that afternoon, quarterbacking one team of relatives and friends against another on which Robert Kennedy called the signals. That same day he went for a long walk along the beach with 3-year-old daughter, Caroline.

In Washington, on January 20, 1961, a cold and windy day after a

> . . . On the Friday after next, I am to assume new and broader responsibilities. But I am not here to bid farewell to Massachusetts. For 43 years—whether I was in London, or in Washington, or in the South Pacific, or elsewhere—this has been my home. . . . The enduring qualities of Massachusetts—the common threads woven by the Pilgrim and the Puritan, the fisherman and the farmer, the Yankee and the immigrant—will not be and could not be forgotten in this nation's Executive Mansion. They are an indelible part of my life, my conviction, my view of the past and my hopes for the future.
>
> Massachusetts Legislature, Boston, Massachusetts, Jan. 9, 1961

"Children," President Kennedy said, "are the world's most valuable resource and its best hope for the future."

snowfall, John F. Kennedy took the oath of office. Shedding his overcoat despite the weather, as if impatient with its weight, he delivered an eloquent inaugural address. It was a pledge to uphold freedom throughout the world and an impassioned plea for America to move forward.

As part of the inaugural ceremonies America's most distinguished living poet, Robert Frost, read a poem. Old and wise, he said to the new President as they stood together on the platform in an icy wind, "I hope you will turn out to be more Irish than Harvard!" Jack Kennedy remained both fighting Irishman and intellectual idealist.

A new spirit entered the White House with the Kennedys. It was the spirit of youth and high resolve. President Kennedy brought to the office of President a quick mind and the ability to use the power he had fought so hard to win because he had desired it so intensely. He was steeped in American history, aware of his time in it. He was clear-sighted and well informed. He surrounded himself with trained advisers, many of them from the Harvard faculty. His own mind was agile and controlled. Always in private discussion or in public statement he appealed to reason rather than to feelings.

If a free society cannot help the many who are poor, it cannot save the few who are rich.

Inauguration, Washington, D.C., Jan. 20, 1961

So let us begin anew—remembering on both sides that civility is not a sign of weakness, and sincerity is always subject to proof. Let us never negotiate out of fear. But let us never fear to negotiate. . . .

Inauguration, Washington, D.C., Jan. 20, 1961

With a good conscience our only sure reward, with history the final judge of our deeds, let us go forth to lead the land we love, asking His blessing and His help, but knowing that here on earth God's work must truly be our own.

Inauguration, Washington, D.C., Jan. 20, 1961

. . . Though we like to think of ourselves as a young country— this is the oldest republic in the world. When the United States was founded there was a King in France, and a Czar in Russia, and an Emperor in Peking. They have all been wiped away, but the United States has still survived.

Inaugural Anniversary Dinner, Washington, D.C., Jan. 20, 1962

John Fitzgerald Kennedy was the youngest man ever to be elected President of the United States. In his inaugural address he told the world that the torch had "been passed to a new generation of Americans."

The central fact about John Kennedy was that he wanted terribly to be President and that he loved being President. The intensity of his desire was a measure of the high value he placed on the office. His deep sense of the power, responsibility and dignity of the Presidency and of the demand that it makes for strong leadership showed in his bearing, his statements and his actions. That a gifted man of clear intelligence found the Presidency good made it good. His placing of a high value on the office seemed to make it an office of high value.

If as men and statesmen they have the qualities within them, Presidents develop while in office. The responsibilities and the opportunities as well as the duties insure this growth. John Kennedy had grown at every stage in his career. That growth was accelerated now. The Presidency seemed to ennoble the spirit of John Kennedy, and he seemed to ennoble the office. He could be coldly realistic in political maneuvering, but he held certain ideals. One was his ideal of the America of the future. Another was his ideal of the Presidency.

He had fought for his country in war. He fought now to lead it to a new understanding of itself and a new position in world leadership. The welfare of the entire nation, both within its borders and in the world community of nations, was in his care, and he was deeply aware of it.

His own interests had been in history, in politics and in writing. He learned to know and value other interests and pursuits. Science and the

Nor is it accidental that many of our outstanding Presidents, men such as Jefferson or Wilson or Truman, have had a deep sense of history. For all of the disciplines, the study of the folly and achievements of man is best calculated to help develop the critical sense of what is permanent and meaningful amid the mass of superficial and transient events and decisions which engulf the Presidency. And it is on this sense, more than any other, that great leadership depends.

"John F. Kennedy Tells Youth How to Prepare for the Presidency,"
an article in Parade Magazine, Sept. 23, 1962

Democracy is a difficult kind of government. It requires the highest qualities of self-discipline, restraint, a willingness to make commitments and sacrifices for the general interest, and also it requires knowledge.

Dublin, Ireland, June 28, 1963

These landmarks of Washington, D. C.—the White House, the Washington Monument and the Jefferson Memorial—are symbols of our nation's heritage, a heritage of which President Kennedy was deeply aware.

Eighteen-month-old "John-John" enjoying his first visit to his father's White House office.

rapid development of the space age necessitated new awareness on which to base new decisions. He developed it, and he grew in other directions.

Perhaps in part through the influence of Jacqueline Bouvier Kennedy, he came to be more conscious of the arts—painting, sculpture, poetry, music—and to see them as fundamental and lasting parts of American culture. In his own words, he brought the 20th century into the White House. He also brought art and intellect. Intellectuals were appointed to posts as Presidential aides. There was the urgency of youth, the light of free intelligence and the color and sound of the arts about the Presidential mansion while the Kennedys lived there.

There was also glamour. The young President and his attractive wife, their small daughter, Caroline, and their infant son, John, born just before his father took office, were ideal subjects for pictures, news stories, magazine articles, television and books. Caroline once stole the show at a press conference when she appeared unannounced in a pair of her mother's high-heeled shoes. At another time a delighted photographer came on small John happily at play in the office of the President in the East Wing of the White House while his father worked behind his carved desk. The Kennedy clan of famous father and mother and the many brothers and sisters and their children also drew much attention. Perhaps no other Presidential family was ever as widely publicized to as large and as pleased an audience.

John Kennedy, aggressive but poised and graceful, had about him the unmistakable air of one to the manner born. It cannot be achieved in one generation. It is seldom attained in the three it took the Kennedys to rise from relative obscurity to international prominence. It showed in the way the President looked, dressed and moved, and in his deeply ingrained sense of *noblesse oblige* — the duty to serve others which is the responsibility as well as the right of those privileged by wealth, education and social position. It was an obligation which President Kennedy felt and upon which he acted throughout his public career. Personal ambition was strong in him. So was unselfish devotion.

John Kennedy did not achieve perfection. Few men do. He had no magic wand with which he could make the ills of the world vanish. No man has. Like other men, he was sometimes wrong in his judgments and, like other men, he sometimes failed to accomplish what he attempted.

His Administration suffered a severe blow early. An anti-Castro invasion of Cuba by Cuban exiles trained in the United States had been planned before President Kennedy took office. He gave the orders for the invasion. Lacking strength, particularly adequate air support, the invasion was a disastrous failure. The result was loss of American prestige throughout the world as well as the collapse of the exiles' hopes. Castro and his Russian backers emerged triumphant in this phase of Communism's conflict with the United States.

The Kennedys often enjoyed musical performances on the White House lawn.

President Kennedy's cabinet is sworn in: (l. to r.) Secretary of State Dean Rusk, Secretary of the Treasury C. Douglas Dillon, Secretary of Defense Robert S. McNamara, Attorney General Robert F. Kennedy, Postmaster General J. Edward Day, Secretary of the Interior Stewart L. Udall, Secretary of Agriculture Orville L. Freeman, Secretary of Commerce Luther H. Hodges, Secretary of Labor Arthur J. Goldberg and Secretary of Health, Education and Welfare Abraham A. Ribicoff.

Later a summit meeting with Premier Khrushchev of Russia, on which President Kennedy had placed high hopes for world peace, was ineffectual. That same year Russia flaunted United States protests and built the Berlin Wall separating democratic West Germany from Communist East Germany.

In 1962 a new Cuban crisis threatened. Russia had built missile sites in Cuba, which is only 90 miles from the American mainland. Cuba, armed with Russian missiles seemed to be in a position to wipe out much of American defenses within minutes. Russian military personnel were in Cuba in force. Russian ships were carrying more men and offensive weapons to the island.

President Kennedy addressed the American people directly on television, telling them of the situation, describing what preventive measures had been taken and what still might have to be taken. The United States demanded removal of the missiles and destruction of the Russian missile bases in Cuba. The U.S. Navy blockaded Cuba to prevent passage of arms-carrying Russian ships. American planes and atomic submarines were held in instant readiness. American forces were mobilized. After five tense days Russia gave in and agreed to remove its weapons and men and destroy the missile bases. It was a showdown in which the United States, led by President Kennedy, triumphed.

President Kennedy proved his effectiveness in international affairs in still another dispute with Russia. In September 1961, Russia violated a moratorium under which the testing of nuclear weapons had been halted. Reluctantly, President Kennedy directed American nuclear officials to resume testing in the atmosphere. Two years later in an address at American University in Washington on June 10, 1963, he proposed that efforts be renewed to prohibit nuclear explosions. A new treaty with Russia was drawn up and put rapidly into effect.

During his Administration, President Kennedy met with Soviet Premier Khrushchev.

We cannot escape our dangers—neither must we let them drive us into panic or narrow isolation. In many areas of the world where the balance of power already rests with our adversaries, the forces of freedom are sharply divided. It is one of the ironies of our time that the techniques of a harsh and repressive system should be able to instill discipline and ardor in its servants—while the blessings of liberty have too often stood for privilege, materialism and a life of ease.

But I have a different view of liberty.

State of the Union Address to Congress,
Washington, D.C., Jan. 30, 1961

My fellow citizens: Let no one doubt that this is a difficult and dangerous effort on which we have set out. No one can foresee precisely what course it will take or what cost or casualties will be incurred. Many months of sacrifice and self-discipline lie ahead—months in which both our patience and our will will be tested—months in which many threats and denunciations will keep us aware of our dangers. But the greatest danger of all would be to do nothing.

Television-Radio Address on the Soviet Arms
Buildup in Cuba, Washington, D.C., Oct. 22, 1962

No Cuban need feel trapped between dependence on the broken promises of foreign Communism and the hostility of the rest of the hemisphere, for once Cuban sovereignty has been restored we will extend the hand of friendship and assistance to a Cuba whose political and economic institutions have been shaped by the will of the Cuban people.

Inter-American Press Association,
Miami Beach, Florida, Nov. 18, 1963

This hemisphere is our home and I cannot understand . . . why it is possible for the Soviet Union with one half of the wealth of the United States to put as much resources and money and assistance into the single island of Cuba of six million people as this rich country does in its own back yard for all of the countries of Latin America.

Convention of the AFL-CIO, New York, New York, Nov. 15, 1963

As the country had reason to note in recent weeks during the debate on the Test Ban Treaty, scientists do not always unite themselves on their recommendations to the makers of policy. This is only partly because of scientific disagreements. It is even more because the big issues so often go beyond the possibilities of exact scientific determination.

National Academy of Sciences, Washington, D.C., Oct. 22, 1963

Every time you scientists make a major invention, we politicians have to invent a new institution to cope with it, and almost invariably these days and, happily, it must be an international institution. . . . The ocean, the atmosphere, outer space, belong not to one nation or one ideology, but to all mankind. . . .

National Academy of Sciences, Washington, D.C., Oct. 22, 1963

White House Photo: Abbie Rowe

"If this treaty fails, it will not be our doing," President Kennedy said as he signed the Nuclear Test Ban Treaty.

There were failures and successes of international action under President Kennedy. Despite Communist aggression in Laos and Vietnam, which he tried to contain by preventive military action, most of his policies were effective.

On taking office one of President Kennedy's immediate domestic concerns was for the preservation of America's natural resources. In a special message to Congress in March 1962 he proposed an eight-year program to acquire new Federal lands for purposes of conservation and recreation. He asked for nine new national parks and for increases in the open-space areas held by the states. He asked for further preservation by both the national and state governments of fast-vanishing shore lines and of the remaining American wilderness. The beauty of America's land, lakes, rivers and its coastlines mattered to President Kennedy. He knew and loved the plains and mountains, the waterways and forests of the United States. He wished their beauty to remain unspoiled.

(continued on page 68)

National Park Service Photo: Jack E. Boucher

Our greatness today rests in part on this gift of geography that is the United States. . . .

"Our Commitment to Future Generations,"
an editorial in Country Beautiful Magazine,
Feb.–March, 1964

To a surprising extent, the sea has remained a mystery. Ten thousand fleets still sweep over it in vain. We know less of the oceans at our feet . . . than . . . of the sky above our heads. It is time to change this. . . . A storm along Cape Cod may well begin off the shores of Japan. The world ocean is also indivisible. . . . International scientific cooperation is indispensable if human knowledge of the ocean is to keep pace with human needs.

National Academy of Sciences, Washington, D.C., Oct. 22, 1963

. . . We are reaching the limits of our fundamental needs—of water to drink, of fresh air to breathe, of open space to enjoy, of abundant sources of energy to make life easier.

Pinchot Institute for Conservation Studies,
Milford, Pennsylvania, Sept. 24, 1963

The history of America is, more than that of most nations, the history of man confronted by nature. . . .

From the beginning, Americans had a lively awareness of the land and the wilderness. The Jeffersonian faith in the independent farmer laid the foundation for American democracy; and the ever-beckoning, ever-receding frontier left an indelible imprint on American society and the American character.

Introduction to a book, *The Quiet Crisis*, by Stewart L. Udall,
Holt, Rinehart and Winston, 1963

Jack E. Cole

President Kennedy asked for nine new national parks to preserve the fast-vanishing American wilderness and seashores. Our parks today include Olympic National Park in Washington (above), and (below, l. to r.) Point Reyes National Seashore in California, Cape Cod National Seashore in Massachusetts and Fort Clatsop National Memorial in Oregon.

W. Woodbridge Williams

Jack E. Boucher

Antipollution programs are necessary to insure clean streams and lakes for fishing and recreation.

A stand of sequoia trees, which are among the largest and oldest living things in the United States.

Theodore Roosevelt was one of the great Presidents, John Kennedy said, because he began the conservation movement in America.

It is not always the other person who pollutes our streams, or litters our highways, or throws away a match in a forest, or wipes out game, or wipes out our fishing reserves.

Pinchot Institute for Conservation Studies,
Milford, Pennsylvania, Sept. 24, 1963

The great movements in this country's history, the great periods of intellectual and social activity, took place in those periods when we looked long range to the future. . . . It was in the days of Theodore Roosevelt, when the whole national conservation movement began, and all of the decisions [were made] in a much easier period, when we had far fewer people . . . which makes it possible for us to travel throughout the United States and still see green grass and still have some hope for the future.

I want us in 1963 to make the same decisions here in the United States. . . .

Tacoma, Washington, Sept. 27, 1963

American agricultural abundance offers a great opportunity for the United States to promote the interests of peace in a significant way and to play an important role in helping to provide a more adequate diet for peoples all around the world. We must make the most vigorous and constructive use possible of this opportunity. We must narrow the gap between abundance here at home and near starvation abroad. Humanity and prudence, alike, counsel a major effort on our part.

Washington, D.C., Jan. 24, 1961

Yosemite Park in California. Mr. Kennedy found what was for him an exhilarating new America on his Western conservation tour.

(continued from page 64)

He had called for service to country and for sacrifice to attain the goals he visualized for America. Soon after taking office he proposed the Peace Corps which was authorized by Congress in September 1961. In the Peace Corps, American volunteers are serving as teachers, nurses, engineers and in many other capacities in undeveloped areas of the world. At the same time they are learning to understand other peoples and helping them toward a better understanding of the United States.

President Kennedy did not always succeed as well at home. As skilled a politician as he was and despite his continually growing popularity and prestige, he was unable to get most of the liberal legislation he wished adopted by the Congress.

He had campaigned for a "New Frontier," advocating increased Federal aid to education, medical care for the aged, more civil rights legislation. Later he asked for income tax reduction and other measures designed to improve the American economy. He believed he expressed the wishes of the majority of the American people, but Congress did not agree, and the measures urged by the President did not become law.

On one crucial point President Kennedy did not have to have Congressional approval. The laws already existed under which he was empowered to act. As the Negro push for equal rights increased and dispute arose, particularly about school and college integration, President Kennedy insisted on equal treatment for all Americans. When necessary, he sent troops to enforce integration. As a schoolboy he would never give in once he was convinced that he was right. He was convinced that he was right now. He knew his stand would cost him votes in another election, but he could not and would not compromise. He was unflinching in his stand on civil rights.

Wide World

Mrs. Kennedy chatting with children from around the world at a State Department benefit.

. . . The overseas success of our Peace Corps volunteers, most of them young men and women carrying skills and ideals to needy people, suggests the merits of a similar corps serving our own community needs: in mental hospitals, on Indian reservations, in centers for the aged or for young delinquents, in schools for the illiterate or the handicapped. As the idealism of our youth has served world peace, so can it serve the domestic tranquillity.

State of the Union Address to Congress,
Washington, D.C., Jan. 14, 1963

Thousands of Americans are serving throughout the world in the Peace Corps started by President Kennedy.

Peace Corps Photo: Rowland Scherman

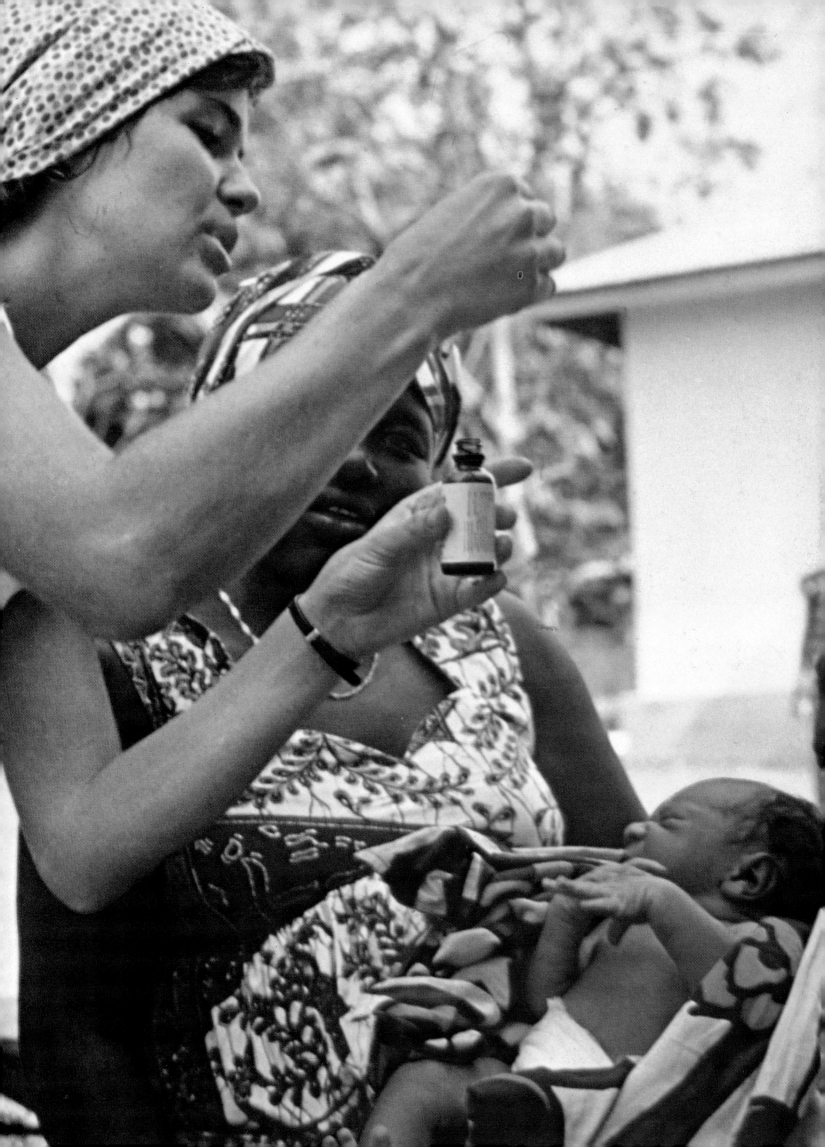

Abraham Lincoln—a man who fought for his ideals—was one of President Kennedy's heroes.

President Kennedy followed no set principles of policy. He tried to make decisions on the basis of the facts, then do what he considered practical and right. His heroes among American Presidents—George Washington, John Quincy Adams, Abraham Lincoln, Andrew Johnson, Chester A. Arthur and Theodore Roosevelt—were men who had thought and fought for themselves. From boyhood the best that he was and could do had been demanded of him. He gave his best now. Impatient of Government red tape, he often cut across channels to deal directly with the men concerned with an issue rather than with official departments. He had a habit of doing things himself, often following through on details of a kind which many Chief Executives delegate to those under them.

Always he played to win, whether it was football, a political campaign or a war. He fought down physical pain, even playing golf, which he enjoyed, though every swing at the ball jarred his damaged back. He could disguise it under a relaxed, informal manner, but his intensity was never far below the surface. He could antagonize as well as charm. His self-confidence could sometimes seem to be arrogance. He was cordial but he was by nature reserved. Sometimes in the cool detachment of his appraisals he seemed to lack inner warmth, but it was there.

The very night after the election, after his opponent had conceded and he had made his acceptance speech to the nation from the armory in Hyannis, he invited all the newspapermen who had been with him on the campaign to his home for an informal get-together. One humorously remarked that he now had something in common with a President. He too had an injured back. Quickly the new President was serious. He asked detailed questions about the newsman's injury. When he had the answers he went off to another part of the big house and telephoned his own doctors long-distance. He made appointments for his newspaper friend, then ordered his own plane readied to fly the reporter to the appointments. It was almost a half hour before he returned to his other guests and the beginning of his new responsibilities.

> . . . The Emancipation Proclamation was not an end. It was a beginning. The century since has seen the struggle to convert freedom from rhetoric to reality. It has been in many respects a somber story. . . . Despite humiliation and deprivation, the Negro retained his loyalty to the United States and to democratic institutions. He showed this loyalty by brave service in two world wars, by the rejection of extreme or violent policies, by a quiet and proud determination to work for long-denied rights within the framework of the American Constitution.
>
> Emancipation Day Message, Washington, D.C., Sept. 22, 1962

The Kennedys were admired throughout the world for the dignity and charm they brought to the White House.

After the orbital flight of Lieut. Col. John H. Glenn Jr., President Kennedy described him as "the kind of American of whom we are most proud."

"What fun you must have!" he would say boyishly, almost enviously, to an astronaut or a pilot or someone else brought to the White House for recognition of some outstanding achievement. Sometimes as President he must have envied other people their simple freedom.

Hyannis Port was always home, and he was there as often as he could be during the summer and until late in the fall. One morning in the summer of 1963, a young Hyannis housewife was shaking her dust mop out the side door when she saw a familiar big gray convertible slip through a winding lane and ease toward her down Sea Street from the Port. His thick, reddish-brown hair bright in the sunlight and tossing in the salt wind, the President waved and flashed a conspiratorial smile as he shot past. She waved her dust mop in return.

"Jack just went by all alone!" the young woman called happily to her husband. She was glad he had been able to escape for a little while.

For greater privacy the President and his family lived that summer in a big house on Squaw Island across a short causeway from the Kennedy Compound, but people knew of his coming and going when the helicopters from Otis Air Force Base in Falmouth dropped down on the lawn in Hyannis Port or took off. The Kennedy houses were brightly lighted at night when he was at home. You could be sure of seeing him every Sunday morning when, usually holding Caroline by the hand, he came into Hyannis for 10 o'clock Mass at St. Francis Xavier. A place was always roped off in the parking lot for the official car of the President and that of the Secret Service, but before he came in or went out the side door of the church he always stretched across the ropes to shake hands with the waiting crowd of visitors and townspeople.

This was his home. These were his friends. Among them were those who had been grown men and his friends when he was a boy. Several

I believe yesterday we saw an interesting contrast in the response which Colonel Glenn made as to whether he had prayed, and he said that he had not, that he had made his peace with his Maker many years before, and the statement made by Titov in which during his flight, as he flew over the Soviet Union he realized, he said, the wonders of the Communist system.

I preferred Colonel Glenn's answer because I thought it was so solidly based, in his own life, in his activities in his church, and I think reflects a quality which we like to believe and I think we can believe is much a part of our American heritage. . . .

Presidential Prayer Breakfast, Washington, D.C., March 1, 1962

were now old and ill. Without fanfare, with no publicity, the President went to see them as often as he could when he was at home. He was loyal in his affections.

President Kennedy sometimes seemed aloof. Even as a boy he had always seemed to keep something of himself to himself. Strangers and even close friends were often aware of this quality which seemed part of his inner integrity. The outer aloofness disappeared when he was with children. Children trusted him instinctively, and he had no distrust of them.

A few nights after he had been elected, one of his close friends and neighbors at Hyannis Port gave a party to celebrate the victory. There were perhaps 150 men and women there, all happy for him, all his friends. Many had known him for most of his life. Some could remember him as a scrawny small boy in torn shorts and a faded sweatshirt. He had always been "Jack" to them. Suddenly he was "Mr. President" and one of the most powerful men on earth.

People felt ill at ease. The talk was stilted and stiff. No one seemed to know quite what to do or what to say. Suddenly the 5-year-old daughter of their hosts appeared in the doorway. Spotting the one person in the room, other than her parents, who was important to her, she rushed up to him, arms out, with a happy cry of "Mr. Kissable!" For some reason it was what she had always called him.

Jack Kennedy swept her up and dropped into the nearest chair with her in his lap. "Oh, I'd like to be around 10 or 15 years from now!" he told her. From that moment the party was warm and human.

Many times the President picked up all the small Kennedy children and every other child in sight, piled them into his motorized golf cart, and took them to the local shop for ice cream and cold drinks. At other times he would load them all into the Marlin and take them for a short cruise about the bay. Hyannis Port's children were almost as concerned as he when Caroline's beloved Welsh terrier, Charlie, spoiled pet of the neighborhood, was badly ripped and chewed up by a larger dog. The President dropped everything to rush Charlie in his own car to the

Pix

The President and his gracious wife and daughter, Caroline, were an engaging, charming family.

Children are the world's most valuable resource and its best hope for the future. It is a real tragedy that in an era of vast technological progress and scientific achievement millions of children should still suffer from lack of medical care, proper nutrition, adequate education, and be subjected to the handicaps and uncertainties of a low-income, substandard environment.

Washington, D.C., July 25, 1963

animal hospital. Young Hyannis Port rejoiced when Charlie recovered.

John Kennedy loved the Cape. He loved many other things. He was proud of his Navy service. His dress sword hung on the wall. The coconut shell on which he had scratched his message from Nauru Island was on his desk. Just outside his office he hung, with what seemed almost equal pride, the certificate awarded him by a gardening club for his skill in developing the gardens on the South Lawn of the White House.

He had many honorary degrees. Harvard made him a Doctor of Laws in 1956. The citation was to John Fitzgerald Kennedy, "brave officer, able Senator, son of Harvard." He was elected to the Harvard Board of Overseers the following year. Other universities delighted to honor the young President.

On October 26, 1963, he went to Amherst College in Massachusetts for the ground-breaking ceremonies for a library to be named for Robert Frost, who had died earlier in the year. At a special Presidential Convocation, Amherst bestowed another LL.D. on John Kennedy, pledging its support, applauding his skill, honoring his courage and leadership.

It was an old story to the President, but no one would have thought so. He was too vital, too much interested, too seriously concerned with poetry

(continued on page 78)

It is my judgment that there is no career that could possibly be open to you in the 1960s that will offer to you as much satisfaction, as much stimulus, as little compensation perhaps financially, as being a servant of the United States Government.

I think within all of us, and really in a sense, I suppose endowed almost by nature in addition to a natural desire to advance our own interests, there is also a parallel desire, and that is to be part of this great enterprise of public service. The totalitarian powers have exploited that. Even in Cuba Mr. Castro's emphasis, certainly at the beginning, was on a desire to improve the lot of the Cuban people. In China we had all of these examples of people spending their days off going out on illiteracy, health, building dams, doing all the things to build a better country. This is in all of us.

I think that it is a more difficult and subtle problem in a democracy, with a great deal of emphasis, of course, on individual liberty, on the right of pursuing our private interests, and so on, so that while there is this desire, frequently it does not have a chance to express itself. But the desire is there. . . .

To Participants in the Summer Intern Program for
College Students, Washington, D. C., June 20, 1962

N.A.S.A.

Tiros I, the first weather satellite. Mr. Kennedy knew the benefits to be derived from space research.

. . . Robert Frost was one of the granite figures of our time in America. He was supremely two things: an artist and an American. A nation reveals itself not only by the men it produces but also by the men it honors, the men it remembers. In America, our heroes have customarily run to men of large accomplishments. But today this college and country honors a man whose contribution was not to our size but to our spirit, not to our political beliefs but to our insight, not to our self-esteem, but to our self-comprehension. In honoring Robert Frost, we therefore can pay honor to the deepest sources of our national strength. That strength takes many forms, and the most obvious forms are not always the most significant. The men who create power make an indispensable contribution to the nation's greatness, but the men who question power make a contribution just as indispensable, especially when that questioning is disinterested, for they determine whether we use power or power uses us. Our national strength matters, but the spirit which informs and controls our strength matters just as much. . . . Robert Frost coupled poetry and power, for he saw poetry as the means of saving power from itself. When power leads man toward arrogance, poetry reminds him of his limitations. When power narrows the areas of man concerned, poetry reminds him of the richness and diversity of his existence. When power corrupts, poetry cleanses. For art establishes the basic human truths which must serve as the touchstone of our judgment. The artist, however faithful to his personal vision of reality, becomes the last champion of the individual mind and sensibility against an intrusive society and an officious state. The great artist is thus a solitary figure. He has, as Frost said, a lover's quarrel with the world. . . . This is not a popular role. If Robert Frost was much honored during his lifetime, it was because a good many preferred to ignore his darker truths. Yet in retrospect, we see how the artist's fidelity has strengthened the fiber of our national life.

If sometimes our great artists have been the most critical of our society, it is because their sensitivity and their concern for justice which must motivate any true artist, make him aware that our nation falls short of its highest potential. I see little of more importance to the future of our country and our civilization than full recognition of the place of the artist. If art is to nourish the roots of our culture, society must set the artist free to follow his vision wherever it takes him. We must never forget that art is not a form of propaganda; it is a form of truth.

Amherst College, Amherst, Massachusetts, Oct. 26, 1963

President Kennedy once said of the late poet Robert Frost (right), "Because of Mr. Frost's life and work . . . our hold on this planet has increased." They are pictured at a ceremony with Massachusetts Senator Leverett Saltonstall (second from left) and Secretary of the Interior Stewart L. Udall.

(continued from page 75)

and education and what both can mean to the country. He was relaxed and at home in the atmosphere of intellect where he had proved that he belonged. He spoke with understanding of Robert Frost and poetry, saying that he saw "little of more importance to the future of our country and our civilization than full recognition of the place of the artist."

John Kennedy said he looked forward to an America that would have mind as well as muscle, grace and beauty as well as strength, insight and wisdom as well as power. He cherished beauty allied to intelligence. He valued excellence.

The President spoke easily at Amherst, lighting his words with humor that did not hide his seriousness, flashing his radiant smile. A professor of history, sober in his black doctor's gown worn for the occasion, looked at him in pleased surprise. "He acts as if he is enjoying himself," he said.

He was. He was President of the United States. He was alive, fully alive. He was happy in the expression of his distinctive talents. He had accomplished much but, charged with promise yet unfulfilled, it seemed that he would accomplish more, much more.

President John Fitzgerald Kennedy was assassinated in Dallas, Texas, on November 22, 1963.

I think politicians and poets share at least one thing, and that is that their greatness depends upon the courage with which they face the challenges of life. There are many kinds of courage—bravery under fire, courage to risk reputation and friendship and career for convictions which are deeply held. Perhaps the rarest courage of all— for the skill to pursue it is given to very few men—is the courage to wage a silent battle to illuminate the nature of man and the world in which he lives. . . .

Recorded for the television program, "Robert Frost: American Poet." (CBS) Feb. 26, 1961

There are many kinds of strength and no one kind will suffice. . . . Above all, words alone are not enough. The United States is a peaceful nation. And where our strength and determination are clear, our words need merely to convey conviction, not belligerence. If we are strong, our strength will speak for itself. If we are weak, words will be of no help. . . .

To have been delivered at Dallas, Texas, Nov. 22, 1963

John Fitzgerald Kennedy valued excellence. He devoted himself unselfishly to the Presidency.

A man may die, nations may rise and fall, but an idea lives on. Ideas have endurance without death.

Opening of the new USIA transmitter complex
at Greenville, North Carolina, Feb. 8, 1963

. . . There is a quotation from Lincoln which I think is particularly applicable today. He said, "I believe there is a God. I see the storm coming and I believe He has a hand in it. If He has a part and place for me, I believe that I am ready."

We see the storm coming, and we believe He has a hand in it, and if He has a place and a part for us, I believe that we are ready.

Presidential Prayer Breakfast, Washington, D.C., March 1, 1962

Photographs by George P. Koshollek Jr.
for the Milwaukee Journal

*President Kennedy was
buried at Arlington
National Cemetery on
November 25, 1963.
Right: Mr. Kennedy's family
leaving the Capitol.*

Above: Funeral cortege with traditional riderless horse. Left: View of the Lincoln Memorial from Arlington National Cemetery as cortege crosses Potomac River. Below: Changing of guard at grave after the funeral at Arlington National Cemetery.

Cornell Capa: Magnum

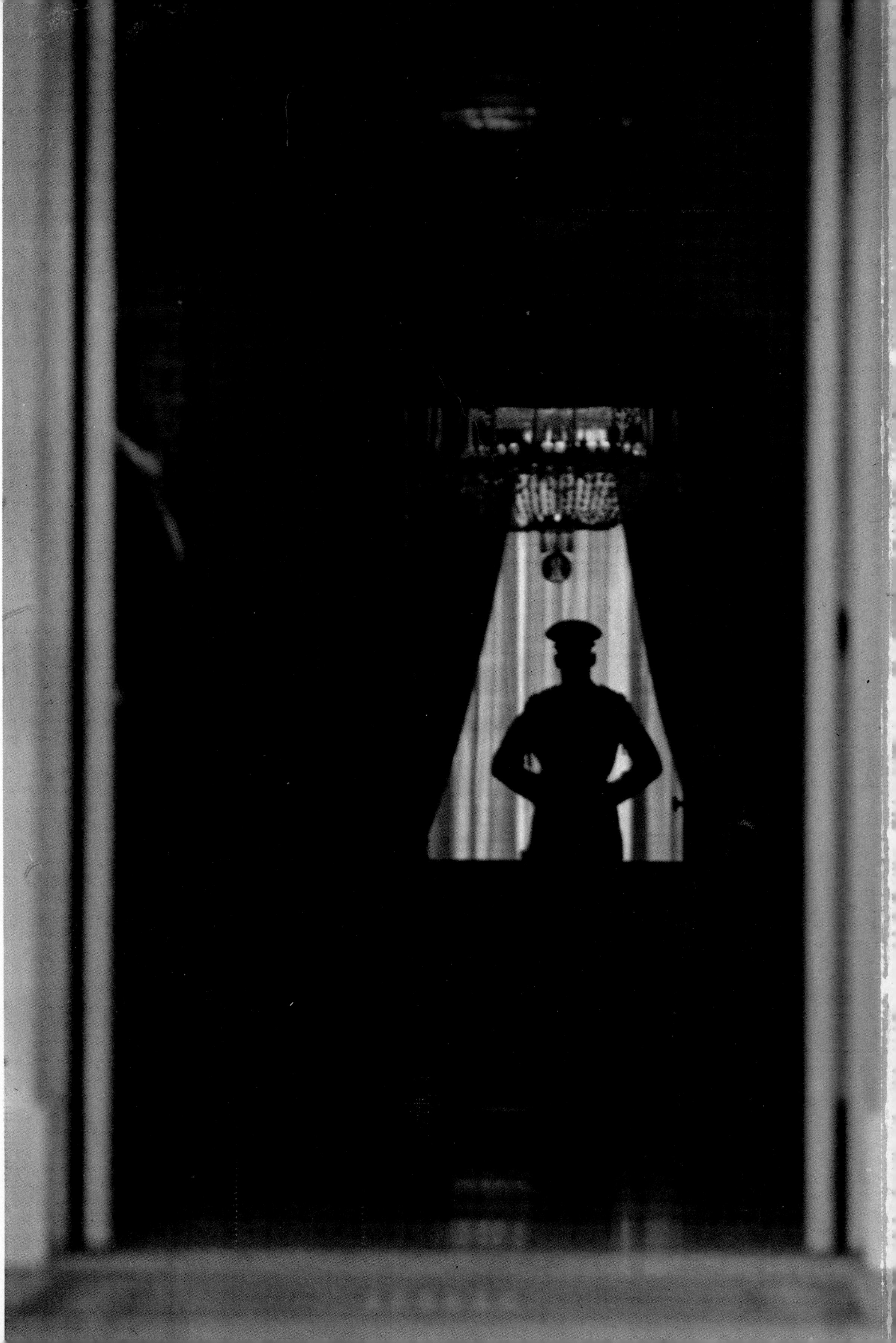